T0110525

Cambridge Elements ≡

Elements in Digital Literary Studies
edited by
Katherine Bode
Australian National University
Adam Hammond
University of Toronto
Gabriel Hankins
Clemson University

THE CHALLENGES OF BORN-DIGITAL FICTION

Editions, Translations, and Emulations

Dene Grigar
Washington State University
Mariusz Pisarski
*University of Information Technology
and Management in Rzeszow*

CAMBRIDGE
UNIVERSITY PRESS

Shaftesbury Road, Cambridge CB2 8EA, United Kingdom

One Liberty Plaza, 20th Floor, New York, NY 10006, USA

477 Williamstown Road, Port Melbourne, VIC 3207, Australia

314–321, 3rd Floor, Plot 3, Splendor Forum, Jasola District Centre,
New Delhi – 110025, India

103 Penang Road, #05–06/07, Visioncrest Commercial, Singapore 238467

Cambridge University Press is part of Cambridge University Press & Assessment,
a department of the University of Cambridge.

We share the University's mission to contribute to society through the pursuit of
education, learning and research at the highest international levels of excellence.

www.cambridge.org
Information on this title: www.cambridge.org/9781009507370

DOI: 10.1017/9781009181488

© Dene Grigar and Mariusz Pisarski 2024

This publication is in copyright. Subject to statutory exception and to the provisions
of relevant collective licensing agreements, no reproduction of any part may take
place without the written permission of Cambridge University Press & Assessment.

When citing this work, please include a reference to the DOI 10.1017/9781009181488

First published 2024

A catalogue record for this publication is available from the British Library.

ISBN 978-1-009-50737-0 Hardback
ISBN 978-1-009-18147-1 Paperback
ISSN 2633-4399 (online)
ISSN 2633-4380 (print)

Additional resources for this publication at http://www.cambridge.org/Grigar_Pisarski

Cambridge University Press & Assessment has no responsibility for the persistence
or accuracy of URLs for external or third-party internet websites referred to in this
publication and does not guarantee that any content on such websites is, or will
remain, accurate or appropriate.

The Challenges of Born-Digital Fiction

Editions, Translations, and Emulations

Elements in Digital Literary Studies

DOI: 10.1017/9781009181488
First published online: February 2024

Dene Grigar
Washington State University

Mariusz Pisarski
University of Information Technology and Management in Rzeszow

Author for correspondence: Dene Grigar, dgrigar@wsu.edu

Abstract: *The Challenges of Born-Digital Fiction: Editions, Translations, and Emulations* addresses the growing concern about how best to maintain and extend the accessibility of early interactive novels and hypertext fiction or narratives. These forms of born-digital literature were produced before or shortly after the mainstreaming of the World Wide Web with proprietary software and on formats now obsolete. Preserving and extending them for a broad study by scholars of book culture, literary studies, and digital culture necessitate they are migrated, translated, and emulated – yet these activities can impact the integrity of the reader experience. Thus, this Element centers on three key challenges facing such efforts: (1) precision of references: identifying correct editions and versions of migrated works in scholarship; (2) enhanced media translation: approaching translation informed by the changing media context in a collaborative environment; and (3) media integrity: relying on emulation as the prime mode for long-term preservation of born-digital novels.

Keywords: Digital Preservation, Born-Digital Literature, Media Translation, Emulation, Migration, Collection

© Dene Grigar and Mariusz Pisarski 2024

ISBNs: 9781009507370 (HB), 9781009181471 (PB), 9781009181488 (OC)
ISSNs: 2633-4399 (online), 2633-4380 (print)

Contents

Introduction: Welcome to the Funhouse!

The box measures 6.25 by 9.25 inches and is skinned in a shiny black finish and silver lettering that reads "Uncle Buddy's Phantom Funhouse" and "a hyper-media novel by John McDaid" (Figure 1).

Removing the box top, you see two audio cassettes, each containing musical compositions (the first by someone named Buddy Newkirk and the second by an Art Newkirk); a letter from Chris, who appears to be an editor of a magazine called *Vortex*; a copy of a science fiction story written by Buddy and edited by Chris; a twelve-page manual, a one-page installation guide; a registration card – and five 3.5-inch floppy disks. It is 1993, and though you are familiar with hypertext narratives having previously read Michael Joyce's *afternoon, a story* and Stuart Moulthrop's *Victory Garden*, you have never encountered one packaged in a box and with so much physical media associated with it. So, you read the manual and learn how to install the work. After a few minutes of your Macintosh Classic whirring and beeping, the work launches, and you land at the opening screen where you encounter a bitmapped image of a house. Mousing around the image, you realize it is an interactive map with hyperlinks leading to various spaces in the house. During your exploration of these spaces, you also learn the box you opened earlier constitutes the literary estate of *your* Uncle Buddy. You are not told what happened to him, but in order to find out, you must continue to explore the house with its many strange and wondrous rooms, listen to the music cassettes, and read the short story and editor's letter.

Welcome to McDaid's *Uncle Buddy's Phantom Funhouse*. The work was published in 1993 on HyperCard 2.0 on the floppy disk format and on CD-ROM later that same year by Eastgate Systems, Inc. Since the release of MacOS X 10.5 in 2007, however, it has been inaccessible to the public. An emulated version that runs easily in the Mini vMac environment was made available in 2017 via download from the Internet Archive, but this version does not include any of the physical media or mention they exist. While fans of McDaid's interactive novel may cheer about their ability to read the work again, this version – disconnected from its contextualizing components – leads us to wonder how readily readers of the emulated version can piece together the mystery of Uncle Buddy's disappearance without listening to the cassette, "The Story of Emily and the Time Machine" or reading Newkirk's "Tree," a story about a man led astray by a mysterious tree. On a visceral level, we wonder about how the loss of the physical media impacts our experience with the work. Obviously, the floppy disks serve as storage for the novel's digital elements, the words, and images that comprise the story. That there are five of them – each containing vital parts of the story as well as programming instructions the

Figure 1 Image of the box containing McDaid's *Uncle Buddy's Phantom Funhouse.*

computer needs to display the story on the screen – means loading all disks to read the novel. Sliding the disks in and out of the floppy disk drive, looking at the work on the screen, clicking the words and images with the mouse to make the screens change, listening to the audio cassettes, thumbing through the letter, story, manual, and instructions all require our senses to apprehend the story and, ultimately, solve the mystery. The box itself, referred to by the author as "the chocolate box of death" (McDaid, "Interview Part 2," 2015), introduces at the outset the story's conceit – what is left of the literary estate of *your* Uncle Buddy – thereby quickly immersing you into the story before you even load the first disk into the drive. Thus, the box and its contents suggest the entirety of the work and conspire to imbue meaning to it.

The Element's Focus

Our Element, *The Challenges of Born-Digital Fiction: Editions, Emulations*, and *Translations*, examines activities, approaches, and strategies underlying the preservation of born-digital literature – that is, art and expressive writing – like McDaid's. Drawing upon platform and code studies, archival theory, translation studies, and media theory, it addresses the growing concern among digital preservationists about how best to maintain and extend the accessibility of works created for hardware and with software no longer supported by contemporary computing systems and which often include contextualizing packaging and physical media that extend beyond what is traditionally recognized as "the work."

The born-digital literary works used as case studies in this Element were produced before or shortly after the mainstreaming of the World Wide Web with proprietary software and on formats now obsolete. Some are works of net art that relied on coding practices, like Java Applets, that are no longer supported by contemporary browsers. In all cases, preserving and extending born-digital art and expressive writing for a broad and sustained study by scholars of book culture, literary studies, and digital culture necessitate these works are migrated, emulated, and ultimately translated for a new audience – yet these activities can impact their integrity and readers' experience. Thus, this Element centers on three key challenges facing such efforts: (1) media integrity: relying on emulation and migration as prime modes for long-term preservation, (2) precision of references: identifying correct editions and versions of emulated and migrated works in scholarship, and (3) enhanced translation: approaching translation as "media translation" informed by the changing context in a collaborative environment during the process of emulating and migrating media. In sum, the Element argues that when the emulation and migration of born-digital media translate the work's code, it also impacts the edition and version outputted in the process and potentially our experience with the work.

Theoretical and Philosophical Underpinnings

Because in this Element we often speak about objects and codes (digital, material, aesthetic) and formulae that let us migrate objects and codes from one environment to another, a good starting point would be to offer a definition broad enough to embrace any codes and any objects. For this we turn to media philosopher Vilém Flusser, who asks us to consider media as the means of expression specific to communication. Such means, Flusser argues, are "structures (material or not, technological or not) in which codes function." Codes are understood in this context as communication codes between sender and receiver that let us orientate ourselves in the media that surrounds us. According to this broad concept, media are not only technologies and means of expression that are taught in media departments of our universities, but also that which can be applied to "the classroom, the body, or even football" (Zielinski, Weibel, and Irrgang 2016: 268). Flusser's commentators identify two main classes of media: Those where the codified message flows from the memory of a sender to the memory of a receiver and those where codified messages are exchanged between different types of memory. The first class of media is discursive media, and the second class is dialogic media. Examples of the first category are ads and the cinema; stock market and a public village square represent the second (270).

The type of discursive media reflected in this Element are *digital* media. If one applies Flusser's definition of media as structures in which codes function in the digital realm, a further distinction is needed. Turning, therefore, to media theorists Jay David Bolter and Richard Grusin, we see a focus on technological objects, such as "[t]elevision, film, computer graphics, digital photographs, and virtual reality" (1999: 65), an approach echoed by Lev Manovich (2001: 8–9). Taken together, the use of the word "media" in "media translation" – as a form of enhanced translation that goes beyond the linguistic – makes perfect sense because digital preservationists migrate and emulate objects and media.

As Nick Montfort reminds us, code is the distinguishing feature of born-digital media (Manovich 2021: 45). The conversion of media, like hypertext literature and net art that rely on code, from one format to another that takes place during migration and emulation is called transcoding, which is, according to Manovich, "the most substantial consequence of the computerization of media" (2001: 45). Along with a distinct "computer layer," associated with "process and packets . . . sorting and matching; function and variable; computer language and data structure," Manovich also argues for the "cultural layer," which he links to "encyclopedia and the short story; story and plot; composition and point of view; mimesis and catharsis, comedy and tragedy." He reminds us that the two layers "influence each other" or are "composited together" and that "to 'transcode' something is to translate it into another format" (2001: 46–47). He also says that "[n]ew media thus acts as a forerunner of this more general *cultural reconceptualization*" (our emphasis, 2001: 47). In his comparison between old and new media, Manovich says that "[d]igitalization inevitably involves a loss of information. In contrast to an analog representation, a digitally encoded representation contains a fixed amount of information" (2001: 49).

The processes of transcoding, one of the main characteristics of the language of new media, point to internal processes that happen on each of the various levels of digital media, from low to high level of programming languages, from back-end to front-end. Remediation, on the other hand, defined by Bolter and Grusin as a process of one medium being represented in another medium, referring to external, or even a universal dynamic of the development of media through history, is not limited to digital media (1999: 11) and, so, does not rely on code for media transformation. It is worth mentioning another perspective on media that brings forth its *poietic* (generative and creative) potential: According to Polish semiologist Edward Balcerzan, we can only speak of a medium if it can constitute at least one autonomous genre (1998: 15).

The close relation between medium and genre can lead to useful, practical categorization within the history of a given medium that demonstrate their material and aesthetic contacts: audio books, interactive fiction, Instagram poetry, image macro memes – these are examples of genres produced by different media yet entangled in broader processes such as transcoding and remediation. As we will show in this Element, *media* translation is one of such processes.

Because the born-digital literary works discussed in this Element were all produced during the period of time when digital network media developed into what Philip Auslander calls "the cultural dominant" (2008: 23) and potentially "displace[d]" previous modes of communication and ultimately the way humans interacting with them think (Bolter 1991: 1–3), our view toward the human experience with born-digital literature is grounded on a set of premises.

First, knowledge is embodied, and meaning is "always a matter of relatedness" (Johnson 1987: 177). In talking about the embodied schema focusing on containment, Mark Johnson says, "We are intimately aware of our bodies as three-dimensional containers into which we put certain things (food, water, air) and out of which other things emerge (food and water wastes, air, blood, etc.) . . . . In other words, there are typical schemata for physical containment" (1987: 21). He goes on to delineate what he calls "entailments or consequences," including responses to external forces, limits/restrictions, fixity, accessibility, and transitivity (1987: 22). We can say that it is not enough to recognize the containerization of other objects but instead to make sense of them and understand them. Johnson says that "*understanding is the way we 'have a world,' the way we experience our world as a comprehensible reality* (author's italics). Such understanding, therefore, involves *our whole being* – our bodily capacities and skills, our values, our moods and attitudes, our entire cultural tradition, the way we are bound up with a linguistic community, our aesthetic sensibilities, and so forth" (author's italics, 1987: 102). He ends the book with this statement:

> *[M]eaning is always a matter of human understanding, which constitutes our experience of a common world that we can make some sense of. A theory of meaning is a theory of understanding. And understanding involves image schemata and their metaphorical projections, as well as propositions. These embodied and imaginative structures of meaning have been shown to be shared, public, and "objective," in an appropriate sense of objectivity* (author's italics, 1987: 174).

"Meaning is thus always a matter of relatedness" (1987: 177).

Second, the embodied human container relates to the world (and other containers) through its sensoria; it is how we think. By sensoria, we mean the vast comport of modalities that includes sight, hearing, touch, haptic, kinesthesia, kineticism, taste, smell, and proprioception. In her introduction to *Sensorium* Caroline A. Jones tells us that "[t]he human sensorium has always been mediated." Expanding on this statement she argues, "[T]he embodied experience through the senses (and their necessary and unnecessary mediations) is how we think" (2006: 5). Moreover, Francisco J. Varela, Evan Thompson, and Eleanor Rosch remind us that "human experience [is] culturally embodied" and the knower and known, mind and world, stand in relation to each other through mutual specification or dependent coorigination" (1993: 150).

Third, conceptualizing relations between containers involves interacting with other containers and results in various levels of feedback that enable connections and disruptions. Citing Maurice Merleau-Ponty's work, Varela, Thompson, and Rosch tell us that "perception is not simply embedded within and constrained by the surrounding world; it also contributes to the reenactment of this surrounding world. The organism both initiates and is shaped by the environment." They are "bound together in reciprocal specification and selection" (1993: 174). This idea is echoed by N. Katherine Hayles, who argues that cognition is a process of interpreting information "*in contexts that connect that information with meaning*" (author's emphasis 2017: 26).

Fourth, because approaches to preserving born-digital literature that take the work out of its original context through migration and emulation have the potential to disrupt the human experience with the work as well as maintain the connection to it, it is important for the integrity of the process to find a balance between the two.

Fifth, we follow Merleau-Ponty's assertion that indeterminate and contextual aspects of the perceived world are positive phenomena that cannot be eliminated from the complete account of reality. A digital object of art, just as any work of art, is perceptible not only through our structures of understanding, but also through structures on the more material, sensorial level. Sensing, for Merleau-Ponty, is a form of "living communication with the world" (Merleau-Ponty 2012: 53) that enhances our perception through meanings and values that refer essentially to our bodies and lives (Toadvine 2019). Although the work of art belongs to a domain of symbolic activities, from the vantage point of the embodied mind, the sphere of sensing needs to be fully integrated into the sphere of second-order structures that it informs. For Merleau-Ponty these second-order structures belong to the "spiritual," but for a literary scholar they represent the level of interpretation and a wider cultural context that the work is placed by the scholar as a result of interpretation. Because pre-Web digital literature engages our perceptual experience – as we argue – in a more visceral fashion than contemporary digital objects, its "sensing" dimension should inform not only its interpretation, but also migration and preservation efforts. In other words, because the work of born-digital literature is both an object and a process (Bouchardon and Bachimont 2013) in our interpretation and in an effort to preserve the work to future generations, a range of accompanying "disclosures," which Merleau-Ponty finds inexhaustible (Toadvine 2019) – need to be accounted for, at least to an extent that satisfies the preservationists and brings a fuller knowledge and experience of the work to its new reader.

Media translation, one of the main topics of this Element, is a process concerned with "structures in which codes operate" that focuses its attention neither on text nor on representation. In other words, its concern is not language or even the content of storytelling, but rather the totality of modes and media objects that need to be considered while making the effort to migrate born-digital literature from source to target configuration of modes and media. Apart from focusing on code and its various layers that inform the process of versioning and emulation, preservationists direct their attention to other extra-linguistic elements, such as sensorial phenomena that accompany the reading of digital works. These additional effects are a direct result of the embodiment implied in the reading of born-digital literature, the engagement of not only of the user's attention and imagination, but also of motoric, haptic and other "nontrivial" actions. If in addition to interactivity the author of digital work addresses the reader via nondigital surfaces, such as material paraphernalia, as in *Uncle Buddy's Phantom Funhouse*, the extra-linguistic part of the message is even more important.

The nonlinguistic factors of media translation put the preservationist in an interesting position, not only as the translator or curator of the work, whether published in "purely" digital form or as a hybrid of digital and analog materials, but also as a curator of the experience of the work who is fully aware that the conduit of such experience is not only the reader's imagination but also the body. If one wants to search for a theoretical framework that could inform the work of preservationists that target experience of the work instead of the work itself, it would involve reader-response theory, cognitive poetics/narratology, and the new materialism. All these fields of inquiry turn away from the prominence given to language and representation to identify other aspects of human and nonhuman experience as equally important in cultural communication. As such, they can deliver a necessary context for the digital preservation efforts by focusing on phenomena outside of text, whether in the reader's mind or in the material components and relations that entangle the text with the material-discursive forces (Barad 2003: 810). The rethinking of translation and preservation efforts might start, for example, with the basic understanding of anthropologists that inform cognitive approach to literature. Peter Gärdenfors reminds us for example that human beings have been communicating long before language and that in terms of evolution language is a very recent addition to our abilities (Gärdenfors 2006: 120). Following such leads, cognitive narratology searched for elements of nontextual communication that literary storytelling delivers in the text itself by using point of view techniques in nondirect narration, internal monologues and stream of consciousness (Fludernik 2001: 621). Cognitive narratologists identified special intersubjective mechanisms of narration, such as sensory focalization, that refer directly to the readers' sense of smell, taste, touch (Rembowska-Płuciennik 2012: 189).

Born-digital literature, such as *Uncle Buddy's Phantom Funhouse*, make the sensory side of literary communication even more important. This is achieved through amplifying point of view techniques through the second-person narrative, providing user interaction with the text and its objects, and evoking signals from hardware and physical artifacts. The range of sensory communication in born-digital literature has extended, and their potential is much greater than in print fiction because of the much larger number of feedback loops between the work and the reader. The job of a media translator is to migrate these feedback loops and convey the sensorial information they generate to new audiences.

If the text that flickers on the computer screen is not the sole object of media translation, it is neither solely the sphere of bodily interactions nor the sphere of internal workings in the mind of the reader. All these shape our meaning making and interpretation. Johnson proved that physical bodily interactions influence the very way we think by way of metaphorical projections of spatial, motoric categories into language and thought (1987: xiv). However, in the case of digital work deeply entangled with its material conditions and extensions, a distinctive form of a reversed projection takes place. Just as image schemata are figurative extensions of physical and bodily realm into language, the material conditions of digital work form a reversed projection of language, the content of story that is being told, into its context. Hardware and software become material support of the work, and material and multimodal artifacts function as its semantic extension. One can treat that mechanism as a direct result of digital materiality. It works in reverse of image schemata that cognitive poetics speaks of because it does not project sensory information into the domain of thought (to form an extended organizational metaphor), but the mechanism takes elements of the conceptual domain, a theme, voice of the character, elements of storyworld imaginary and distributes them into different registers of the digital-material hybrid that the computer, the material surfaces, and the resulting reading environment create. This digital-material configuration becomes a type of embodied material metaphor that conveys the work's meaning. In the case of McDaid's *Uncle Buddy's Phantom Funhouse* the units of user interaction, *actemes* (Rosenberg 1996: 22), create their embodied meaning by the entanglement of the digital text with material spheres of hardware, printed paraphernalia, and analog media.

Just as media translation cannot be text-centered, it also affiliates itself with a nonrepresentational approach to communication that encourages both preservationists and translators to focus on things rather than words, on material artifacts rather than pure concepts. Such "agential realism" that identifies cultural objects as specific material configurations of the world, and the resulting philosophy of the body and "entanglement" of matter and meaning (Dolphijn, van der Tuin 2012: 15), constitute a valid model for media translation of born-digital literature discussed in this Element. Born-digital literature and its complex materialities can serve as a cultural reservoir for contemporary reflection on human and nonhuman agents in contemporary discourse. However, there are accounts that are even more affiliated with media translation's approach to digital objects that will always be as close to the work, the text, and their material affordances. Ian Bogost in his *Alien Phenomenology, or, What it's Like to be a Thing* projects object-oriented ontology's interest in things onto the realm of digital cultural artifacts, such as software and computer games. Things and objects, according to Graham Harman, are in conversation with each other, where they "witness one another and each contributes to the consistency and coherence of all" (Harman 2005: 95). Thanks to their ability to form relations with other objects, things are able to contain other things, "erupting infernal universe within" (95). Bogost, thanks to his experience as a game developer, is able to test these insights on digital things and objects. The results are fascinating and quite relevant to the subject of this Element. The cultural and computer levels intertwine in Bogost's approach to computers in the context of his version of object-oriented ontology that he rebrands as "flat ontology" (2012: 9).

None of the ontological instances of the computer game that Bogost analyses is one single E.T. Rather, as with every object of digital art, it is all these instances at once, best perceived as an orchestrated blend of interconnected ontologies. Every work we discuss in this Element has exactly the same, or almost the same status. Every time the code of a work changes at one of its levels a new version is created and a new configuration of the work's "ways of being" appears. When a version is acknowledged on a discursive level, by publisher for example, and recognized as a separate object, a version gives way to an edition further complicating the initial state of the original. The work of a media translator and digital preservationist is to track, oversee, and – if needed – initiate such transformations for the benefit of cultural circulation. The main goal of such work and the processes it entails is the accessibility of the work to new audiences.

Our Methodology

The methodology used for our project is grounded in practice-based research that goes "beyond the crafting of words" and involves "embodied interactions with digital technologies" (Hayles 2012: 19). In that context, both authors have been involved in the activities outlined here: migrating and emulating interactive texts, organizing them into versions and editions, and translating them to assure their long-term accessibility. They use the knowledge they have gained through this experience as the foundation of the theories and perspectives expressed in this Element.

Grigar's research is centered in the lab that she founded in 2011 – the Electronic Literature Lab (ELL). One of a handful of media archaeology labs in the United States, it is used for the advanced inquiry into the curation, documentation, preservation, and production of interactive media, specifically born-digital literature, net art, and games. Working with her is a team of scholars, programmers, digital preservationists, designers, and videographers – faculty who teach, and staff and alums who received their degrees in Digital Technology & Culture, a degree program she oversees at Washington State University Vancouver. Additionally, some of the preservation projects outlined in this Element, specifically Sarah Smith's *King of Space* and Thomas M. Disch's *Amnesia*, are undertaken by graduating seniors pursuing this degree as their capstone projects and overseen by the lab's staff. This ecosystem of creative digital thinkers and producers come to their theory and practice with the assumption that computers are not a tool that help us to achieve our goals but rather the medium in which we work. This digital way of thinking frees us from the constraints of print culture and the modes of thinking, processes, and practices built for and in response to it.

Pisarski's research is located at the intersection of the practice and theory of digital literature. As a founder of the Polish online journal *Techsty*, which promotes digital storytelling, hypertext fiction, and digital humanities as a method of critical inquiry, he has led numerous collaborative translations of hypertext fiction and poetry generators, and digital adaptations of literary classics. As a member of the Intersemiotic and Intermedial Lab at University of Warsaw, Pisarski's research combines the findings of digital semiopoetics (a semiological perspective proposed by Ewa Szczęsna) and new materialism with the practice of migration and translation. From this perspective, he sees the performative aspects of the digital sign and its emphasis on experience and embodiment influence not only our tools and artistic expression but also the way we think and our engagement with literary tradition. Entanglement and interconnectedness of digital objects with matter, on the one hand, and discourse, on the other, make the work of translators and preservationists a challenging, but rewarding, quest.

The wealth of media generated during our preservation activities has been developed into a multimedia book built on the Scalar platform and keyed to the specific chapter topics they address. So, while the print book contains seventeen black-and-white images, the multimedia book holds many full-color images, video clips, visualizations, sound files, and animations that further underscore our arguments. Collaborating as we are doing on both a print book and an accompanying digital publication requires the kinds of activities Hayles outlines as once confined to the sciences but now is needed in the digital humanities (2002: 19).

Section Contents

Section 1, "Emulation," looks at the use and value of emulation as a method of preserving born-digital art and literature but goes a step further to argue that a work's extra-linguistic elements, such as sensorial phenomena and physical media affected by emulation, can impact the human experience with the work. To address this challenge, we suggest an approach that considers each work's key features individually and then apply multiple presentation methods based on them. Case studies include editions of early hypertext works, including Judy Malloy's its name was *Penelope*, produced on the Storyspace platform, and McDaid's *Uncle Buddy's Phantom Funhouse* and Stuart Moultrop's *Hyperbola: A Digital Companion to Gravity's Rainbow* and Dreamtime, both created with HyperCard.

In Section 2 "Migration and Translation," we turn our attention to migration and the way in which a work's code and other salient features, such as its presentation and functionality, are translated in the process – a type of translation we call "media translation." We provide several case studies, most notably editions of Richard Holeton's *Figurski at Findhorn on Acid* and Michael Joyce's *Twilight, A Symphony*, to examine the way migration has affected such features as loading screens, multilinks, special navigational keys, and link names and paths. We also look at the Polish translation of Joyce's *afternoon, a story* to illustrate challenges to what we call "radical media translations" that involve both linguistic and media transformations of a text.

Section 3 "Editions and Versions," chronicles the many media translations that have taken place during the thirty-year history of Joyce's *afternoon, a story* to make the case that changes made to a text during such a process result in potentially a new edition and version of it.

Finally, Section 4 "Restoration and Reconstruction: Final Thoughts," lays out a continuum of preservation activities that can be undertaken based on the level of interventions needed to maintain the work's accessibility to the public, starting with documentation and moving to restoration and reconstruction. Numerous examples are presented as case studies, including the restoration of M. D. Coverley's "Fibonacci's Daughter" and the reconstruction of Deena Larsen's "Kanji-Kus," Annie Grosshans' *The World Is Not Done Yet*, Holeton's *Figurski at Findhorn on Acid*, Sarah Smith's *King of Space*, Moulthrop's *Victory Garden*, and David Kolb's "Caged Texts."

This Element is a reflection of many years of preservation activities where emulation, migration, and collection have played large roles in our research. The challenges we have faced as digital preservationists, as we sought to keep these works alive, have resulted in a perspective of this activity that is paradoxically broad in use of the methods available to us and specific in their use. We hope the lessons learned will be useful to others who also care about our digital cultural history.

1 Emulation

At first glance, the interface and structure of the 1990 Edition of Michael Joyce's *afternoon, a story* published for Macintosh computers on floppy disk and the 1990 Edition emulated via the Mini vMac application appear to be the same (Figure 2). The aesthetic associated with early Eastgate works, what Hayles calls the "Storyspace School" (Hayles 2007), is maintained throughout. Readers would encounter the same yoni launcher icon, the double loading screens, the bitmapped image Joyce produced with MacPaint, the gray screen background throughout the 354 lexias, pixelated text in Macintosh typeface, and the same linking system with guard fields nudging readers through the storyline. Two main differences, however, lie in speed and size. The floppy disk on a Macintosh Classic II running System Software 7.1 used during the same period the work was published, for example, takes 19 seconds to load the 539 spaces and 950 links; while the emulated version on a 27" iMac running Mac

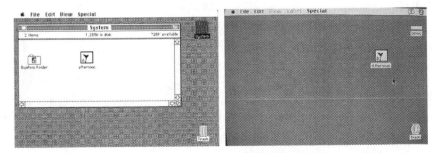

Figure 2 Comparison of the 1991 Edition and emulation of Joyce's *afternoon, a story.*

OS X 15.13.6 (High Sierra) zips through the loading phase so quickly that it is challenging to log the numbers. Even resetting the speed control of the Mini vMac application cannot match the speed of the emulated version to that of the version on floppy disk. Additionally, on the same legacy computer, the floppy disk version fills the screen keeping the eye directly fixed on the work, while the emulated version accessed on the iMac with its 27-inch screen is swamped by space afforded by it. In fact, it would take six interfaces of the emulated version of *afternoon: a story* to fill the screen of this desktop.

Despite these differences, emulation figures as the preferred method of preserving digital media by many digital preservationists. In "The Myth of Immateriality: Presenting and Preserving New Media," for example, Christiane Paul lays out the three paths to preserving works whose hardware and/or software have become obsolete, with emulation figuring as the most optimum among the more "inelegant" solutions as collecting legacy software and hardware and potentially "problematic" migration (2007: 269).

Emulation and the Reading Experience

Defined as the process of recreating computer hardware with software or "execution of a program written for a different computer, accepting the identical data and producing the identical results" (Butterfield 2016: 550), emulation allows users to run old applications on modern machines when the hardware and software is no longer compatible with the new. Although the job of preserving born-digital literature is increasingly institutionalized, until recently emulation (in service of preservation) was done mostly by authors themselves, by single readers, or by distributed efforts of online communities. McDaid's *Uncle Buddy's Phantom Funhouse*, mentioned in the introduction, and Moulthrop's *Hyperbola: A Digital Companion to Gravity's Rainbow* and *Dreamtime* represent two examples of an emulation developed by the author and distributed via the Internet Archive's Software Library.

Because emulation involves transferring data from its source to a target domain, it constitutes a type of translation. Questions that arise within this context are: What is the data translated in an emulation? Which aspects of data remain intact during transfer, and which are lost? As we will demonstrate, current theories of digital literary translation might not sufficiently account for the participatory, interactive, and experiential aspects of a work of born-digital literature in translation, and it is especially true with emulation. Out of four dimensions of born-digital literary translation proposed by Maria Mencía, Søren Pold, and Manuel Portela (2018) – the translinguistic, transcoding, transmedial and transcreational – only the transcoding dimension is activated, for example, in McDaid's emulation of *Uncle Buddy's Phantom Funhouse*, and only to a certain extent since that work extends beyond the digital with its physical media. Because the core aim of emulation relies on leaving the original code intact and on demonstrating the work as it executes on original software, the change in code refers mostly to the process of repackaging to a dedicated translation layer needed for the emulated work to be correctly interpreted by newer machines. In the case of emulation, changes in code are much less prominent than in other types of transformation, such as media translations discussed later in this Element, when the code quite often needs to be rewritten as it travels from one programming language and system to another. The language, the types of semiotic codes these works artistically employ, and the creative compositional process that support them remain largely intact in emulation. This indicates, firstly, that Mencía, Pold, and Portela's model might be linguistically centered, and, because of this orientation, some crucial aspects of the process of emulation, mainly the experiential ones, are not accounted for.

In his response to Mencía, Pold, and Portela's argument, Montfort acknowledges their model's indebtedness to traditional translation and points out that the only new dimension of born-digital literature translation is transcoding (2019). Paul likewise makes a similar argument in her essay when she reminds us that emulators are "computer programs that 're-create' the conditions of hardware, software, or operating systems, so that the original code can still run on a newer system" (2007: 269). Within the digital realm, the change of code implies the change of a work version. In the case of simulation, it is mainly the code that changes, while the other dimensions – at least from those enumerated by Mencía et al. – remain unchanged. Montfort expands their model to include several additional areas that come into play in the digital work's poetic, material, and social expression. These extra dimensions are metrical, material, and contextual. Metrical dimension, an important aspect of translation, especially when considering rendering of the classical poetry meter into modern languages, comes back to the foreground of translator's attention in born-digital poetry, especially if subjected to computational constraints. As such, it is of not much relevance in the practice of migrating born-digital works across platforms, especially if no linguistic transformation is involved. Material dimension, on the other hand, that points to production aspects of the work, along with its sensory and experiential effects, plays a crucial role in translating media. The contextual aspect is related to the framing of the work in its social context – whether the work is presented in a gallery space, within a specific generic group, or specific platform niche is equally important. As practitioners of the translation of born-digital literature, we need to add another area of translation that relates to the embodiment of the reader in the act of reading: the *experiential* dimension.

We argue that what impacts the experience with an emulated work are the conditions of hardware and software. The new technological context and the disappearance of the original hardware result in a radically altered reading experience. Crucially missing are the sensorial, motoric sensations connected directly to the material context of reading. The feel of the plastic in our fingers as we slide a disk into a drive, the sound of the Macintosh Classic II whir as it reads the disk, and appearance of the disk icon on the gray screen after it loads – these sensations differ from those experienced when accessing the emulation on the 27" iMac with a built-in 2560 x 1440 display and a NVIDIA GeForce GTX 775M graphics card. These phenomena derive from the embodiment of the reader's perception in the sensorial realm of interaction with the hardware and software with their – as Jones puts it – "necessary and unnecessary mediations" (2006:5). When migrating, recreating, or restoring a work of born-digital literature, the intensified interaction between meaning and information must be accounted for. Some of the sensorial components of the narrative discourse might even find their way onto the other side of the migration process. The sphere of sensorium is crucial for reconstructions of born-digital works, but less so in emulation.

While it is true that emulation stands as an important strategy for accessing work created on obsolete hardware and software, emulation alone is not the best method of reconstructing the multisensory presentation of the work that lies at the heart of the experiential dimension. The emulated version of *Uncle Buddy's Phantom Funhouse,* for example, could be better experienced – and perhaps the mystery surrounding the disappearance of the titular character actually solved – if it were accompanied by images of the box and its contents, sound files of the music found on the cassette tapes, and video playthroughs of the work as it was experienced on a legacy computer. The lack of documentation evident in most emulations of born-digital literature – added to the fact that the internal processing of user's input, screen resolution, and the font sizes of the original work can be dramatically different on the host machine – means a faithful recreation of data can bring about an unfaithful recreation of the work to the reader.

Emulating Early Hypertexts

Using examples drawn from early hypertext fiction and Flash net art, we look at examples of emulations to reflect on the ways emulation potentially changes the reader's experience. Specifically, we compare emulated versions with those distributed to the public by publishers or artists themselves, most notably the interactive novel *its name was Penelope* (1993), the HyperCard animated story *Dreamtime* (1992), and the hypermedia novel *Uncle Buddy's Phantom Funhouse* (1993).

Judy Malloy's *its name was Penelope its name was Penelope*, originally published and exhibited during the "Revealing Conversations" exhibition held at the Richmond Art Center in California in 1989, exists in five versions. Version 1.0 was produced in BASIC and published on a 5.25-inch floppy disk for IBM computers. In 1990 Malloy expanded the original version and published Version 2.0 via Narrabase Press. A year later Eastgate Systems, Inc. published Version 3.0 – a retooling of Version 2.0 from the original BASIC program into the Storyspace format distributed on a 3.5-inch floppy disk. A CD-ROM version was produced in 1998 but was not broadly distributed or promoted.[1] Without access to this edition, we cannot know how it fits into the work's edition schema. Upgrades to hardware and software over the next decade drove the creation of Version 4.0, produced by the Critical Code Studies Working Group 2016 from January 18 to February 14, 2016, and called by Malloy "The Scholar's Version." This is the emulation of Version 2.0 that takes its source hardware of the original Apple II/IBM, running a software written in BASIC, into modern machines via the DOSBox emulator (Grigar 2018). A version created as an app for access via an Apple iPad demoed behind the scenes of the Electronic Literature Conference in Paris in 2013 was never completed. A recent iteration however, Version 5.0, released in 2020, is a Web-based version that features some 2D animations with an interface resembling the DOSBox version.

No other work can illuminate the fascinating complexity of emulation, versioning, and media translation of born-digital literature as *its name was Penelope*. The five versions of the work already mentioned have, for twenty-seven years, formed the main core of its multiple iterations in digital and physical realms. We must also mention that, similarly to other projects of Malloy, such as the pioneering database novel *Uncle Roger* (1986–1988), the original idea for *its name was Penelope* originates from the realm of artists' books. This "original version," as the author calls it, used yellow text on a black background and "had a look and feel that reflected its Greek epic origins and sweep" (Malloy 2018). It becomes clear that the goal of the emulation from 2016 was not to recreate these enhanced material contexts that contribute to multiple identities of *its name was Penelope* but rather to reconstruct the core narrative functionalities of the 1990 Narrabase Press version (Figure 3). These functionalities include random access to lexias by pressing the return key – an action on part of the reader that simulated the acts of recollection and associative

---

[1] This edition of the work does not appear on Eastgate Systems, Inc. website. Attempts to find it by using the Wayback Machine have not been successful.

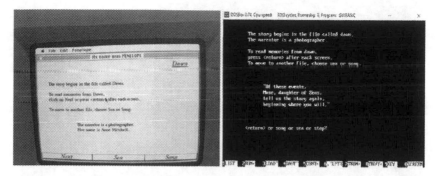

Figure 3 Comparison of the opening screen of Judy Malloy's *its name was Penelope*. On the left, the 1993 Edition for Macintosh produced on the Storyspace platform; on the right, the 2016 Edition emulated with DOSBox.

reflection of the main character – and the thematic threading of selected parts of the work under the labels, such as "song" or "sea," to which readers gain access by direct text input. Yet even such a minimal goal set for the emulation – minimal because we do not expect from emulations to recreate graphics or reinvent the user interface – brings with it heavy losses and differs so much from the original. This DOSBox emulation does not recreate the source work's visual appearance. The font, the text size, and the text input area of the screen are qualities of the original not preserved in the emulation, which itself borrows almost all aspects of the look, feel, and interaction from the bare-bones design of the DOSBox emulator aesthetic, seemingly transparent, and purely functional, yet able to leave its own mark on the emulated work. The mark voids the original not only of its cultural context but also of content that could be used in documentation and preservation, such as basic information about the visual appearance of the original, emulated work. Thus, the DOSBox emulation strategy, somewhat controversially, abstracts the process of emulation, understood as the representation of hardware by software, to a level of pure functionality. No hardware is actually emulated in *its name was Penelope*, just core functions of the original program. Upon its launch, for example, the work appears without other computational elements associated with experiencing it on the computer, like the launcher icon, the loading screen, and such. Conversely, the emulation of *afternoon: a story* in Mini vMac makes it possible for contemporary readers, archivists, and librarians to gain knowledge about the original cultural context of the work – like the way humans interacted with the computer when accessing it and what the original software systems offered for authors that might be used to amplify an artistic strategy. Such knowledge is not explicit, but implied, and can be reconstructed based on the emulation (in service of preservation). The DOSBox model of emulation makes no such knowledge possible to achieve.

One could ask how far the emulation of early, born-digital literature could or should go in order to be informative (about the work itself) and engaging (as a storytelling machine)? The bold, large, fluorescent green letters flickering on the screen of Apple II that might have constituted a strong memory in the minds of the early readers are not part of the work for the new audience for *Uncle Roger*, for example. Returning to *its name was Penelope*, gone is the hum of the small computer, the squeaks of the magnetic reading mechanism when the disk is read by the drive, and potential loading errors that may prevent the text from appearing on the screen. Gone also is the long journey of our fingers when typing words on a huge, heavy keyboard of the PC from the early 1990s. As Malloy herself demonstrated during her Traversal of *Uncle Roger*, published for Apple II, typing in two names of characters in the story in order for the program to display lexias that feature these characters and their interactions is by no means trivial. It takes time and patience (Malloy 2015).

Moulthrop's Hyperbola: A Digital Companion to Gravity's Rainbow and Dreamtime

Hyperbola: A Digital Companion to Gravity's Rainbow (1989) and *Dreamtime* (1992) were originally created in the popular Apple's HyperCard software that allowed for text and graphical animation as well as advanced user interaction, such as creating links between selected "stacks" of content. Like McDaid's *Uncle Buddy's Phantom Funhouse*, these early, self-published works of Moulthrop are held by the Internet Archive's Software Library as a part of the service dedicated to preservation via the emulator of Macintosh System Software 6.0 and 7.0.

However, as an emulation, both works provide an example of what we identify as the most lossless type of transfer, although losses are inevitably made. Because the nature of knowledge is embodied and the information comes to us through different forms of engagement with the world, from linguistic to experiential, the work of born-digital literature should be regarded within its many registers of signification. In same fashion, by accounting for various realms through which the work communicates its message, it needs to be translated, recreated, or migrated. Thus, when comparing different degrees of emulation we should account for changes in the realms of code, language, modalities, materialities, experience, and contexts. Borrowed from the area of digital music and imaging, a lossless emulation, while never *fully* achievable, manages to transfer most of the linguistic, semiotic, modal, poetic, material, or contextual aspects of the work in a way that satisfies the needs of translator, preservationist, and the target audience. A lossy emulation, on the other hand, is one unable to recreate many of these dimensions.

Perceived through this angle, *Hyperbola* does not undergo changes neither in code nor language, nor any of its semiotic modalities (it does not employ audio or video effects). *Dreamtime*, on the other hand, loses an important aspect of sound.[2] In the emulated version, randomly reshuffled voice-over snippets that form meaningful, syntactical sequences, such as *This is not / a trivial / simulation* or *Hypertext / is bullshit / what makes you say that?,* are not heard and, therefore, do not contribute to the meaning of the work. Apart from this crucial difference in modalities, both works, from their original versions to their contemporary emulations, whether on Mini vMac or Basilisk emulator or on a curated site of the Internet Archive, remain solely digital objects. They have no external physical expressions – such as a folio to hold floppy disks or a manual explaining how to install them – outside of the hardware necessary to run them. Within the browser the works are accessible through emulation scripts provided and maintained by the Internet Archive. The format and the version of the files emulated on the host site also do not change; neither does the ecosystem of Macintosh software necessary to run them. *Hyperbola* and *Dreamtime* were written and read in HyperCard software, which remains the fundamental contextual reference. However, there is an important shift in the larger context. The works are presented on a site under Moulthrop's account as a part of the preservation efforts of the Internet Archive, effectively making them part of their "Software Library: Macintosh." The biggest change in these emulations is the disappearance of the original hardware that reappears in the process of emulation in the browser. It is now up to the emulation environment to translate/recreate their expressive qualities. Reading the work ultimately relies on the efficiency of emulation code.

It is worth noting that the sound missing from *Dreamtime* can make its way back to future emulated versions through factors over which neither the author nor the curator may have control, such as updates to the emulation software or updates to browsers on which the software is run. Consequently, even in a case of straightforward migration, when the most significant element lost in the migration is the legacy Macintosh hardware, the experience of the work by new readers encountering it for the first time will be different and limited – that is, "lossy."

McDaid's *Uncle Buddy's Phantom Funhouse*

The loss of material and contextual dimensions of the original that comes with emulation is even more obvious when the original is not a purely digital work

---

[2] The emulated version of *Moulthrop's* Hypercard works we discuss was read on Safari, Chrome, and Opera browsers on the Mac OS Monterey System on 30/03/2022.

and conveys its artistic message through various physical and media objects accompanying the text. Within this context, *Uncle Buddy's*

Phantom Funhouse delivers a great case study. The work's digital core emulated on the Internet Archive forms just a part of the multimodal, hypermedia package. As mentioned previously, the version published in 1993 includes two cassette tapes, proof pages of a short science fiction story, a letter from the editor of *Vortex* magazine, a user's manual, and five 3.5-inch floppy disks comprising the HyperCard stacks. One can say that with audio tapes, booklets, and even the framing box itself, *Uncle Buddy's Phantom Funhouse* effectively constitutes an example of an embodied hypermedia, one that appeals to a broad range of sensoria and experiences that include interacting with the physical media, listening to the tapes, reading the short story and letter, and slipping floppy disks in and out of the drive.

Not surprisingly, its emulated version consisting only of the content hosted on the floppy disks or CD-ROM delivers a dramatically different experience. In comparison, *Dreamtime* changes only on the level of code ("game data," "file list," and "emulator data" run in browsers), with the resulting contingencies in one of its semiotic channels (lack of sound), in its perceived context (the work being part of the preservation project), and on the level of presentation and interaction (screen resolution, processor speed). *Hyperbola*, having not lost any of its modalities, undergoes the minimum amount of change: on the level of experience and context. If one could consider *Hyperbola* as almost lossless, then in comparison, the emulation of *Uncle Buddy's Phantom Funhouse* is drastically lossy. When emulating a work that involves so much physical media, the question we need to ask when emulating it is, "What constitutes a work when the entirety of the materials packaged in the box is intended to provide contextual information?" Considering that the story and letter from the editor reinforce the main fictional conceit in which readers are tasked with finding the truth about the disappearance of their uncle Buddy by exploring the materials packaged in the box, and without them the search may not lead to success, then the answer is clear. A lossless emulation must include all of the media of this hypermedia novel. While a fundamental loss occurs already on the text level, it is the loss of the breath of physical media that presents the challenge. Emulation alone is not able to deliver those additional framing devices.

The Impact of Embodied Experience

Readers and scholars have paid increased attention to the embodied aspects of reading digital fiction, challenging the notion of immateriality of literature made and read on computer screens. Minute material details and sensorial phenomena associated with born-digital literature influence not only emulation protocols but the very approach to the work, bring the awareness of its ephemeral nature, and introduce preservationist traits to the tasks of a media scholar. A recent example of such an approach toward born-digital literature that is sensitive not only to the text on the screen and the narrative discourse empowered by computation but a whole range of experiential triggers comes from Astrid Ensslin's book *Pre–Web Digital Publishing and the Lore of Electronic Literature.* Recounting her experience with *The Eastgate Quarterly Review of Hypertext*, a series of hypertext poetry and fiction published by Eastgate Systems, Inc. from 1993 to 1996 that Ensslin accessed in Grigar's personal library in her lab, she does not start from the title page, or the cover of the edition she's about to read. Rather, her attention, as a reader and scholar, is trained on the material conditions that support the work and sensorial phenomena that surround it. As she recounts about her experience with Volume 1, Number 1, which contains Jim Rosenberg's *Intergrams*:

> The folio covers open with a reluctant pop, as if imploring me to respect their age and leave them untouched. I carefully wriggle out one of the 3.5-inch floppy disks squeezed into the front flap. It has "for Macintosh" printed on its sticky label [. . .] I viscerally recall the sheer delight this noise used to evoke in me decades ago, and I can feel it now as poignantly as I used to a multisensory, haptic rhythm that seems to be shaking the entire body of the computer, and with it, my hands on the worn beige plastic mouse and keyboard. On the downward flickering, black-and-white monitor display a window tells me the software is loading. (Ensslin 2022: 1)

When the same work is run through an emulator on modern machines, it turns into an accelerated stream of "flickering signifiers" (Hayles 2000) channeled through a whole spectrum of semiotic modes enabled by digital media: linguistic communication would still be enhanced by the visual, the auditory, and the performative affordances of the digital sign. Yet much of the experience of reading the work as an emulation is lost.

The superfast text input we perform daily on our modern devices might be much different from the deliberate, slow work on the keyboard required by command line interfaces. As a result, readers need to think twice before committing to a chosen character or narrative key word and before putting it in the command line. Although we cannot advocate for emulations to include all the quaint sensorial sensations that accompany the original reading, there are aspects of the embodied experience of the original that – at least in a model, optimal emulation – should find their equivalents on the other side of the transformation process. Perhaps we do not need to transfer the sounds of the computer ventilator nor the squeaks of floppy disk readers, but why not try to find an interface equivalent to the slow, deliberate text input? Why not create a subtle simulation of the screen flicker or slow down the number of processor cycles per second that the host's machine performs when running the emulation (this feature is found on the Mini vMac emulator already but does not always match the speed of the original, as we have already shown). The understanding of emulation as a way of preservation, documentation, and curation of literary tradition will constantly change and expand its scope based on the emulating technologies at hand and on the perceived goals of emulation. The examples we present prove that these goals should always be set higher than the standard, expected result and reach the function-driven approach into the realm of experience and memory of the original.

Looking at emulated versions of *Hyperbola, Dreamtime, its name was Penelope*, and *Uncle Buddy's Phantom Funhouse*, we see that the phenomenological and cognitive perspective relating to the translation of code, language, modalities, materialities, experience, and contexts are impacted (Table 1). These matter even more than the loss of hardware as they deliver a range of sensory and motoric effects engaging the reader's body in the act of reading.

The table shows six areas of media translation and reflects changes in the areas that take place when the work of born-digital literature is emulated. To better represent migration of the work from one software/hardware environment to another, we had to distinguish three layers of code. The first one is the machine code level; the second is the source code level; and the third, the logical level, which we understand as a set of abstracted rules that govern the algorithm that determines the display of content and the course of interaction (e.g., guard fields). Distinguishing machine code from the source code is useful in

Table 1 Layers of translation in digital media. The x marks major changes during transformation from source to target environment in the case of *Hyperbola, Dreamtime, its name was Penelope*, and *Uncle Buddy's Phantom Funhouse*.

	Code			Linguistic Content	Modalities	Materialities	Experience	Contexts
	M	S	L					
Hyperbola	x						x	x
Dreamtime	x				x		x	x
its name was Penelope	x					x	x	x
Uncle Buddy's Phantom Funhouse	x	x				x	x	x

emulation as the former relates to instructions that the code sends to a specific computer processor; the latter relates to the processes that run the work within the environment made possible by a specific processor and hardware. The aim of emulation is to run the source code, untouched, on nonnative hardware by repackaging and interpreting it on the host machine that speaks a different language. A special interpreter, part of the emulation script on the machine code level, is needed for the original source code to be understood by the host processor. In other words, for the emulation to be successful, the source code needs to be handled by a different machine code, different interpreters, and the container scripts, such as .js and .wasm files in the case of Flash emulation in Ruffle. In emulation the source code remains the same, but the machine code and its interpreter are different.

The linguistic layer is important for emulation in those cases where the emulated content differs from the original content, such is the case with *Uncle Buddy's Phantom Funhouse*, that was published as a compilation of physical and digital media. The loss of the physical media associated with the work results in a less than successful translation since they are needed for solving the mystery.

The area of modalities concern semiotic codes that constitute the born-digital work, such as visual, audio, video, and animation. Quite often a work loses some of its modalities when emulated. As mentioned previously, the sound in *Dreamtime* is lost in the emulated version. However, if we include the material and the experiential levels into consideration, the range of possible modalities could be expanded and refer to semiotic codes triggered in these two contexts. The sound of a spindle motor in the floppy disk drive when it rotates the magnetic content of a disk belongs to a semiotic code that functions in the material context of born-digital literature. The reader's gestures that activate the "wave of Returns" (Joyce 1995: 185) – by navigating a hypertextual work via the default path accessed by tapping the computer's return key – or alert readers to words that are hyperlinks – by typing the Option and Command keys (or what are called the "Tinker and Bell" keys) – belong to a gestural semiotic code, relevant in media translation because it can be hard to recreate in a browser emulation, and even harder when recreating a Storyspace hypertext for touch-screen devices.

In regard to materialities and experiential layers, we see in the case of *Hyperbola* and *Dreamtime*, both born-digital and digital-only works, nothing substantial changes when reading the works at the time of its publishing and decades later as an emulation. However, the experience changes because the in-browser emulation makes it possible to interact with the work in a different interaction mode, without mouse and even without keyboard, using touch equivalents on touch screen devices for example. *its name was Penelope* and *Uncle Buddy's Phantom Funhouse*, on the other hand, originally expanded its artistic message across several materialities, moving from a work contained on physical media to one presented as digital only.

Finally, the contextual area refers to the transfer of those elements that the work acquired upon its reception and accumulated over the years. Should the work be placed in the same, or similar sociocultural context? Within the same discourse? Does it carry some community-driven protocols of its reading, or perception of its original hardware and software, onto the other end of the transformation process? The contextual consideration, which we borrow from Montfort's proposed addition to the model of born-digital literature translation and Grigar and Moulthrop's Pathfinders methodology,[3] both of which fore-ground not so much technicalities of translation process but possible ways in which the work could be presented to its new audience.

The emulation of *its name was Penelope*, which Table 1 renders as less radically altered by emulation than *Uncle Buddy's Phantom Funhouse*, differs from the two other works in one key area that the extended model of born-digital translation does not map. Both Moulthrop's and McDaid's files are read on an emulator that restores the hardware architecture of the classic Macintosh, its system (Macintosh Software System 7.x), and the specific software (HyperCard) on which the work is read. As a result, the interface of the work does not change much. Screen resolution, font choices, graphical layout, and the navigation are preserved. The emulation of *its name was Penelope*, on the other hand, results in an interface that borrows the look, feel, and behavior from the emulated software (DOS) run on a specific system (a Windows machine). The result brings a radical change in the work's aesthetic, as well as ergonomics of the emulation. DOSBox is able to moderately scale to screen resolutions of contemporary machines, the occasional issue with screen's real estate that could be experienced by readers' of the original – and which were documented during Judy Malloy's Traversal of the work in 2018, mentioned previously – which is no longer present. Due to such scalability *its name was Penelope*, in contrast to Mini vMac's emulation of Joyce's *afternoon, a story*, can even work on full-screen mode, bringing this part of the experience closer to the original. However, because the graphical layout and typography are changed and, to large extent, dependent on the emulated hosts' system, the

---

[3] The centerpiece of the "Pathfinders" methodology is the Traversal. This is a performance by the author and readers of a work of born-digital literature that takes place on hardware and with software contemporary with the release of the work, captured on video. Grigar and Moulthrop suggest many different performances through a work in order to provide a broader scope of a work's complexity.

emulation may give an impression of a version that is too detached from the original's time, although functionally improved.

Also missing from the emulation of *its name was Penelope* is the packaging in which it was originally bundled, a feature that cannot be overstated. The vinyl and cardboard folios convey important information about the work. The folio, for example, is made of dark blue vinyl and sports light blue lettering for the author's name and the work's title (Figure 4). The blue of folio's palette harkens to both the narrator's childhood blue sailboat and the adult narrator's blue box that holds her diaphragm mentioned in the narrative. The cover also features an image of a triangle sail on rippling water, evoking the sailboat – "the Penelope" – referenced in the title and that serves as the metaphor for the narrator's childhood, an experience that cannot be returned to but only remembered with much fondness and nostalgia. Thus, folios for early hypertext literature, which resembled thin volumes of books that could be set upon a bookshelf, not only served as breadcrumbs from the world of print to that of the digital, but also convey important information about the work itself. Their loss, when they are part of the original work, decouples the work from its cultural context.

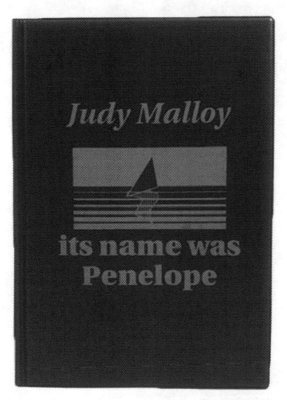

Figure 4 Folio for Malloy's *its name was Penelope.*

2 Migration and Translation

In creating the archival, Web-based version based on the 2001 Edition of *Figurski at Findhorn on Acid* published on CD-ROM for Macintosh and Windows computers, the Electronic Literature Lab created two modes of reading. The first, Classic, retains the look and feel of the work as it was published in 2001. The second, Contemporary, redesigns the interface and functionality for a new audience (Figure 5). One of the first decisions the lab had to make about the design for both reading modes was which fonts to use. For the Classic mode, the team found it could retain all the original fonts that appeared in the 2001 Edition since it utilizes typefaces common to Apple computers of the time – all of which were still accessible to the public in 2021. Decisions relating to the fonts for the

Contemporary mode, however, were not as straightforward since that mode required fonts that fit an updated style. The team made the choice to retain the funky feel of the original title, a decision that led to the adoption of the Adobe font, Cotton. Described as "a mid-twentieth century style casual sans with a vintage t-shirt texture" (Adobe), Cotton – with its letters slightly askew – captures the off-kilter antics of the novel's three main characters who search for a legendary mechanical pig. Fira Sans

Condensed, clean and easy to read, was selected as *Figurski*'s primary font, while Exo 2 supplants Monaco/Consolas for the lexias associated with the Holodeck. Courier was retained for the Terminal. Thus, even though no words of the text or linking strategy were changed, the migration of *Figurski* from CD-ROM to the Web involved making decisions about how best to present the work to a new audience. It involved translating its media.

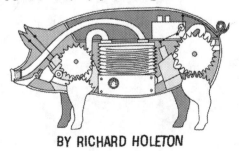

FIGURSKI AT FINDHORN ON ACID

BY RICHARD HOLETON

Figure 5 Interface for Richard Holeton's *Figurski at Findhorn on Acid*, the Web edition.

Media Translation and Its Consequences

Linguistic translation involves the transformation of language, a process that never results in a text *exactly* the same as the original (Biguenet and Schulte 1989: viii). Rather, it reconstructs the total image of a text and the situation conveyed through text via the limiting possibilities of language. As such, linguistic translation requires a study of relationships: between words, between a word and its philological and etymological background, between a word and its cultural ambiance, between a word and its historical tradition, and between a word and its context within a text (1989: xi–xi).

Translating media also involves a process of transformation, but where linguistic translation looks at relationships surrounding words, media translation focuses on "the signifying components" of electronic texts, what Hayles identifies as "sound, animation, motion, video, kinesthetic involvement, and software functionality" (Hayles 2002: 20). Moreover, preserving born-digital literature through the process of migration and emulation involves the translation potentially between formats, software, platforms, hardware, computer languages, and/or digital qualities in a way that impacts the human experience with such works. It may or may not involve linguistic transformation, but always the underlying code is affected and may or may not result in changes to functionality and presentation. The translation of creative media requires the interpretative intervention of the translator and, so, is an act of creation. It may or may not result in transcreation, defined by Cinzia Spinzi as "taking a concept in one language and completely recreating it in another language," a process "generally applied to the marketing of an idea, product or service to international audiences." Because the recreated language is devised to "resonate with an intended audience," the act of transcreation "take[s] translation a stage further [than translation] . . . by letting translators leave their isolation and by requiring a "different mindset to that of translation." Whereas with translation "words such as 'faithful' and 'accurate' are normally used to describe the quality" with transcreation words like "'creative', 'original' and 'bold'" seem to be more common (Spinzi 2018: 6). Taken in this context, media translation is not necessarily centered on transcreative practices although – as the choice of typography in the 2021 version of *Figurski at Findhorn on Acid* demonstrates – it does require creative interventions when the translator determines the most suitable equivalents that can be delivered when migrating the work to her contemporary audience.

The concept of translating media was taken up by Hayles in her book *My Mother Was a Computer: Digital Subjects and Literary Texts*. Here she centers her theory on "physicality, materiality, and embodied textuality"

(2005: 97) to arrive at the notion of "Text as Assemblage" (2005: 105). The shift to thinking about media translation as a transfer from one digital form into another came about as scholars and artists, such as Montfort, Mencía, Pold, Portela, and others, who emulate and migrate works, grappled with the problem of preservation and integrity of the work in the process.[4] Their findings placed relations between code, medium, and language in the center of discussion about translation in the digital realm. Media translation, with examples presented in this Element, shows these relations at play while at the same time foregrounds material and experiential levels of born-digital literature in migration.

The notion of media translation in which linguistic transformations are not in the center of the process but in parallel to other equally important aspects that shape users' experience of the source work marks a radical departure from the traditional notion of translation. Media translation, on the one hand, is concerned with movement between formats, software, platforms, interfaces, hardware, and other attributes of digital communication. On the other hand, it is focused also on our perception of the work that, although mediated by digital phenomena, is also influenced and expressed by material and discursive contexts. From the material standpoint the media translator needs to take into account both hardware related factors such screen size, screen refresh rate, presence of mouse and keyboard, and material artifacts that formed a meaningful part of the original's message. Equally important are discursive qualities that the work accumulates during its reception: frequently shared opinions that become common knowledge and part of the lore surrounding the work, recommended hermeneutic approaches, and reading protocols that accentuate certain practices of reading and interpretation. The additional roles of the translator of born-digital works, who often needs to be the work's editor and agent (Montfort Marecki 2017: i90) media translation extends further into curation and restoration. As we have shown, the importance of hardware-related factors and material artifacts comes into play especially in emulation. With its main goal of emulating hardware with software, emulation exposes limits of migration that identifies its equivalents solely in the digital realm. The emulated version of *Uncle Buddy's Phantom Funhouse*, for example, delivers a different, visibly diminished, experience because the carefully orchestrated set of digital and nondigital signifiers that defined the original is trimmed down to the limited number of digital simulacra. Likewise, the migrated version of *King of Space* differs widely in aesthetic and

---

[4] Montfort rejects the idea suggested by Mencía, Pold, and Portela in their essay "Electronic Literature Translation: Translation as Process, Experience, and Mediation" that there are dimensions beyond the computational.

functionality than the original because vast changes to hardware and software, not to mention audience expectations, necessitated it. Because we define the role, the scope, and the goals of media translation as much wider than particular live implementations, its vocabulary and contexts must be equally wide to include various perspectives on the act of transferring codes from one media container to another. Categories derived from literary studies, translation studies, and media studies might not be sufficient, and one might need to look for additional insights from the fields of cognitive poetics, new materialism, and phenomenology.

The Direct Consequence of Media Translation

Born-digital literature, as expressions of post-Gutenberg media, bring forward aspects of traditional literary communication, such as sound, gesture, and phatic, participatory rhetoric of oral literacies, which technology of print effectively erased by putting a written word in its center. This "secondary orality," which Walter Ong originally attributed to the medium of television (Ong 1982: 133–134), is significantly amplified in digital media and forces preservationists to attune themselves with multi-modalities of contemporary poetics and storytelling. With it comes a shift of perspective: the unit of migration and emulation and the basic element on which one determines a version or edition is often not a single sentence, paragraph, or section, but a gesture that combines a work of the computer code, a scripted interaction of the user and multimodal registers of the work. As such, it projects the translator's task into a realm of performative and sensory phenomena, away from a printed page and closer to a theatrical stage, a shift aptly illustrated by the titles of pioneering research into the impact of digital media on storytelling, such Brenda Laurel's *Computers as Theater* and Janet Murray's *Hamlet on the Holodeck*. Importantly, the unit of media translation points to a performance not only that of the user, but also of the code, which can self-perpetuate its movements in never-ending loops on the stage, or an "event space" (Aarseth 1997: 114) of the work. Rosenberg proposed to rebrand the unit of signification in digital poetry and fiction from the traditional *sem* (a single unit of meaning) to *acteme* – a unit of action (Rosenberg 1996: 22). In many cases, as we will demonstrate, translating a digital work is a process of migrating and recreating *actems* from the original software and hardware to their equivalents contemporary to the translator. Together with multimedia assets and scripts of the computer code that determine the interaction, *actems* form a multilayered bundle of attributes that define the translated media object and inform the result of media translation.

Gesture as a unit of translation brings media translators back from a language-only approach to material aspects of the work that go much beyond print paraphernalia of its different editions. The materiality of the work is expressed on many levels, from software and hardware dependencies tied to socioeconomic contexts of digital communication, to the various ways a digital work can enter the material and physical space in order to be viewed, read, and experienced. Hardware and software, text and its multiple surfaces form a space of exploration and embodiment filled with sensory phenomena that inform the author's context when creating the work and the environment of the reader who experienced the original within the same technological milieu. It is virtually impossible to recreate such a complex setting of interconnected elements in a different time and place. However, some corporeal and sensorial effects of born-digital literature can be partially reconstructed or at least alluded to on the level of assets, scripts, or *actem*s. Recreating the experience of the art object as the event associated with the object and not the object itself has been a part of curatorial efforts in museums and art spaces. The affiliation of art curatorship to the curatorship and preservation of born-digital literature might not be initially obvious. However, the multimodal nature of digital art, the shift from interpretation to action (from *sems* to *actems*), the performativity of code, and the engagement of the user's body – which is often a condition for the work to proceed – make such affiliation a natural part of media translation.

One can approach such decision-making problems from the level of interface. Alexander Galloway defines the interface as an expression of incompatibility between two planes that the interface mediates between (Galloway 2012: viii). The few examples drawn from the experience of the ELL's Live Traversals of early hypertext literature documented on hundreds of video recordings reveal points of incompatibility between the work, with its built-in protocols of reading, and the reading audience habits and expectations at the time of Traversal. In the case of historical software and hardware, one might expect the scope of incompatibility to change over time and render many functions of the interface unreadable by new audiences. Apart from becoming more prominent, interface incompatibility can also diminish over time. On original Macintosh computers from 1989 to 1991 the loading panel with hypertext statistics could stay on the screen for close to a minute for large works. Macintosh computers from the late 1990s shortened the loading time to several seconds. On modern machines – where most Eastgate Systems, Inc.'s classic hypertexts can be displayed only via emulators – the loading time takes just a fraction of a second, and the screen is barely noticeable. The latter case convincingly supports the ELL's application of the Pathfinders methodology for the Live Traversals to be performed on hardware from the time of a work's commercial release. Yet even the closest historical approximation of the techno-logical milieu of the source text might not in itself provide clear answers as to which elements should migrate to new contexts and be included in media translation.

Attributes of Pre-Web Digital Literature

In order to introduce some form of standardized evaluation potentially inform-ing translatological decisions, let's take a step back from the domain of interface into the three-tier domain of code, text, and discourse viewed from user experience perspective.

Loading Screens

One of the first visual elements of the born-digital literature produced on the Storyspace platform that readers encounter after inserting the disk into the disk drive and activating the executable file with the click of their mouse was a loading window that displayed the hypertext statistics, such as number of nodes and links while the work was being loaded on screen. For readers of these early hypertexts, the loading screens relayed valuable information. The number of "spaces," for example, signals how many screens of texts readers could potentially encounter, not unlike the experience of looking at the thickness of a book to determine how much reading the book will entail. Additionally, the number of "links" reveals how intricately woven and complex a hypertext is. Joyce's 1991 Edition of *afternoon, a story* has 539 spaces and 950 links, while Moulthrop's 1991 Edition of *Victory Garden* is close to double the amount of screens with 993 spaces and is structured with three times the number of links, 2804. Many of us who read *Victory Garden* on a Classic II remember walking away from the computer to get a cup of coffee while the computer finished the long loading process.

Because such a feature is no longer a common reading experience, both on and off the Web, the loading screen drew the attention of younger readers participating in ELL's Live Traversals who were unfamiliar with it. It also provoked comments from authors themselves who in many instances were encountering their works in their original environment for the first time in decades. This is not surprising. After decades of advances in reading interfaces on the screen, in education, in entertain-ment, or in public services, contemporary audiences are able to compare and appreciate experiential and pragmatic features of the printed book and born-digital work. By sheer amount of practice and daily use of text-driven applications, they are also competent enough to compare digital reading surfaces with one another. In this context the loading screen of early hypertext literature presents itself as a type of a smart, dynamic index, a framing device that introduces the reader to work by presenting few important data points: number of nodes, number of links, paths, and "key words." Because hypertexts did not feature a typical index of contemporary eBooks, known from Amazon Kindle or Apple Books, an index that is on its own a remediation of its print predecessor, the loading screen was the first and – sometimes – the only expression of the metatextual apparatus that would let readers orientate themselves about the scope, length, and depth of the work they were about to read. So far only one project, the 2021 Web edition of Holeton's *Figurski at Findhorn on Acid*, has reconstructed a semblance of this narrative device to capture this important touchstone of the period.

Emulation engines that try to read born-digital literature using the computational resources of the host machine (a modern PC) render the loading screens of hypertext fiction in an unnatural fashion. Because the host's processor speed is much faster than on the machine the original work was supposed to be read, the speed of the loading of the text statistics makes not only the content of the loading screen unreadable, it also renders it barely noticeable due to the fast-paced processing of the loading data. Contrary to such unwanted result, the reconstructed loading screen visible after clicking the begin button of both the Classic and Contemporary modes of the Web edition of *Figurski at Findhorn on Acid* presents its content in a readable way with the numbers of lexias and links loading just at about the pace they did load on original Macintosh computers of 2001 when the work was published. The recreated feature represents a welcome nod to the earlier stages of digital literary culture and its reading interfaces (Figure 6). At the same time, it also conveys a story of a media translators' connection with the original work together with the level of their attention to detail. For an untrained eye, a seemingly "aesthetic" feature that might express rather a sentimental than functional value is in fact a recreation of an important narrative device, and – at the same time – a telling sign of a media translation made from the heart.

Multilink

Storyspace maps and conditional links constituted a major highlight of born-digital literature. As instrumental elements of a work that influence interpretation and reading experience, they are migrated in the process of restoration or reconstruction. There were, however, narrative components that preservationists of today might judge as less important. One of them is the multilink. Although indeed a minor element of authoring arsenal of Storyspace, not even mentioned as a separate, autonomous feature in the Storyspace User Manual but rather a result of the system-wide response to link creation process, the multilink pointed to an important and forgotten affordance of pre-Web writing. It was the freedom to link anything to anything by stacking one link

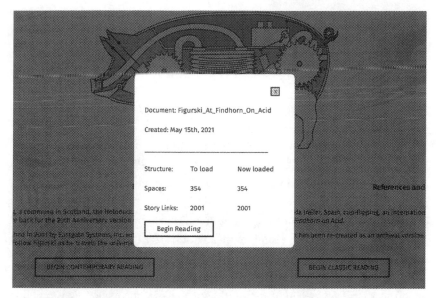

Figure 6 Simulation of the loading screen for Figurski at *Findhorn on Acid*, Web edition.

on top of another. Hardly imaginable in contemporary standards of Web and app design practice, pre-Web writing environments allowed authors to create a link on a word, then another link on a sentence with that word (with a different destination), and then another on an even bigger portion of text that itself led to yet another direction. Storyspace was able to handle these layered links and present them to readers as a menu of available destinations when the word, phrase, or paragraph anchoring the link was clicked. Joyce's *Twilight, A Symphony* featured several examples of such multilinking strategies. They all point to huge flexibility that the hypertext tool offered. Joyce could link one phrase to one particular lexia, and later decide that the same phrase, or the sentence or paragraph that contained it, might as well lead to yet another lexia, or even to several ones at the same time. A resulting new connection would be established and presented as a choice. One lexia, entitled "Cent mille de facts," contains fifteen destinations tied to it and built into a two-layered stack. One link is anchored on a single phrase "what once was a swan," and fourteen more are anchored on the text of the whole content, fourteen verses of a sonnet inspired by Stephane Mallarmé. When clicking on the phrase "what once was a swan," a menu with all fifteen links is shown. When clicking anywhere in the text, outside of that phrase, a menu of fourteen links is visible.

The Web by default promotes one-directional linking of a source to one specific target. HTML specification supports neither bidirectional linking,

a concept promoted by early hypertext theorists such as Ted Nelson (1987),[5] nor
the multilinks on a single anchor. The first attempt to bypass the limitations of
HTML and implement advanced linking strategies in literary projects was made
by experimental poet Robert Kendall, one of the most prominent pioneers of
digital poetry. Author of *A Life Set for Two* (1996) a stand-alone animated poem
published in *The Eastgate Quarterly Review of Hypertext*, Kendall experi-
mented on many available platforms and formats, from HTML to Visual
Basic and Flash. His JavaScript Connection Muse, an authoring toolkit published in 2002, intended to bridge the gap between pre-Web and Web writing by
introducing advanced linking methods of the stand-alone systems to the Web.
The Connection Muse, designed for handling large, or "organic," hypertexts on
the Web (Kendall 2000), featured conditional links, random links, and multilinks. Apart from narrative examples that demonstrate the system, Kendall used
these exotic links in his own Web poetry, for example in *Penetration* (2000).
Significantly, though, the poet and developer does not try to emulate multilinks
of Storyspace. The version of multilinks for the Web developed by Kendall is
closely tied to conditional and random link scripting. As he writes:

> To create a MultiLink, you specify a number of alternative destination nodes
> for the link using the MultiLink Tool. You can then specify that the destin-
> ation should be chosen randomly or according to whether or not certain
> conditions are met. / . . . / MultiLinks can randomly take the reader to a new
> destination. This can be useful if you want to achieve a highly fragmented
> style along the lines of, say, one of William Burroughs' "cut-up" novels.
> (Kendall 2002)

Although the multilink tool is available for authors, it is not designed to be
visible on the reader's side, for example, as a list of available destinations, but
rather these options are already determined by the reading history. In other
words, the first migration of the multilink happens mostly on the author's side,
not on the reader's. With Kendall's Connection Muse the multilink of rich
hypertext structures from stand-alone environments made its way into the
Web and into the hands of aspiring hypertext poets.

   The first direct translations of the multilink functionalities of Storyspace
appeared with the online versions of Joyce's *Twilight, A Symphony*. Just like
in the case of Connection Muse, the solution to commodify the exotic feature on
the Web was delivered through JavaScript. A multilink function reads additional elements of the HTML "href" attribute – such as data-href1, data-href2 –

---

[5] When comparing the Web's handling of documents and interrelations Ted Nelson argued that
"Serious electronic literature (for scholarship, detailed controversy and detailed collaboration)
must support bidirectional and profuse links, which cannot be embedded; and must offer facilities
for easily tracking re-use on a principled basis among versions and quotations" (Nelson 1999: 1).

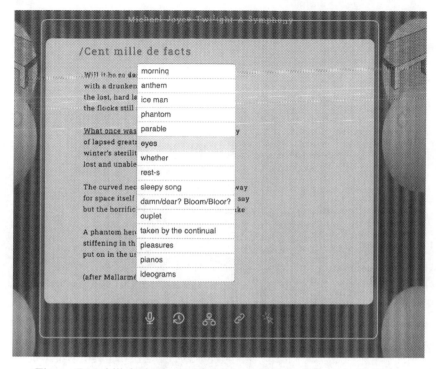

Figure 7 Multilinks in the 2022 Edition of Michael Joyce's *Twilight,*
A Symphony.

to point to alternative destinations and, then, present them in a list populated by
a second set of additional elements of the href attribute: data-tile1, data-title2.
When a link is clicked, a list of alternative destinations appears:

This image shows the list of available destinations displayed by the multilink
panel over a sonnet in the lexia "Cent mille de facts." (Figure 7) The translated
multilink does exactly what the original did: When clicking anywhere in the text
outside of the highlighted phrase, a menu appears with fourteen destinations that,
as readers might guess, correspond to the fourteen lines of the sonnet structure.
Clicking on the only visible phrase renders a list of fifteen destinations. The
stacking of link anchors, although not directly transferred to HTML, is recreated
and reconstructed. Just as in the original, the default sequence triggered by the
enter key is blocked. An error sound is triggered when pressing the "Enter" key on
the keyboard, and readers need to actively engage in choosing a destination.
Because "Cent mille de facts" is an important lexia, with eight other lexias leading
into it, without the migration of the multilink several functional aspects of the
original, not to mention the depth and the scope of attention to detail the hypertext
author paid to the linking functionalists, would be lost.

Tinker and Bell Keys

As mentioned previously, some aspects of pioneering born-digital literature emerged to the foreground of the reader's experience only decades after the original publication. It happens when the function or the meaning of an element, especially if it belongs to the areas of navigation, interface, or a visual display of the text, becomes detached from the standards and habits of new audiences. In these cases, such elements not only are exotic for new users but also become exotic to the original audience or even authors themselves when revisiting the classic works, especially when these works become inaccessible for decades.

Along with the loading screen, the "Tinker and Bell keys," is another exotic feature of many works of early hypertext literature published on the Storyspace platform that surprised readers participating in ELL's Live Traversals. These are, on a Macintosh computer, the OPT + CMD keys that, when held down together, will evoke a box around words noting them as hyperlinks, known in hypertext lore as the Tinker and Bell keys (Grigar 217: 216). On the Web, links are commonly marked by default as underlined, colored portions of text. Before the Web such visual link labeling was not possible. (Macintosh computers did not support color until Macintosh System Software 7.x in 1991.) Inculcated as contemporary readers are with hyperlinking strategies of the Web, experiencing them only after pressing a specific key combination effectively defamiliarizes the experience with the text and forces a slower, more focused, exploration. During ELL's Live Traversals between 2015 and 2021 authors of hypertext fiction admitted that they encountered their works for the first time in years. Inevitably, when preparing to read the work on the original software and hardware, questions about how to make the links visible would be raised and a discussion about the Tinker and Bell keys would follow.

The mechanism of making text link anchors to appear in text is important for multichoice narrative, but it is even more crucial when links are introduced in illustrations. In Kathryn Cramer's *In Small and Large Piece*s, to proceed with the reading and discover more portions of the story, readers need to activate hotlink areas marked on illustrations. In line with events in the story, where the shattering of a mirror serves as a major event and organizing metaphor, the links on illustrations are marked along an organic, unordered pattern, just as small and large pieces of glass would scatter. The use of the Tinker and Bell keys is needed already at the beginning of the hypertext to move along in the narrative. The image on the title screen contains ten possible paths readers can follow in the story, plus two more about the publisher and author. If no OPT + CMD keys are used, readers click anywhere on or off the image, and the work proceeds in a random order. This method of navigation occurs further in the text as well. For example, in the lexia "eye," an image of an eye is divided into eight sections, each hyperlinked to a unique lexia. Simply mousing over the image does not evoke a link; one must use the OPT + CMD keys to access them (Ensslin 2019).

Faced with an element of a reading interface, such as the link highlighting mechanism of early hypertext fiction, a preservationist needs to examine the role that such an element served in the original. The resulting preservation methodology can range from treating the component as a heritage feature, important within the discourse surrounding the specific work or the genre it belongs to but not essential for the reading experience or how it may contribute to the meaning of the work. When reconstructing Holeton's *Figurski at Findhorn on Acid* the lab decided to retain the Tinker and Bell keys as a nod to the work's status as a classic pioneering Storyspace hypertext. However, in the original 2001 Edition, the author introduced his own, custom method of navigating across the grouped content in the form of a Navigator window. There are no hot links on images and the presence of text links, although noticeable, is superseded by the curated traversals of paths offered by the Navigator. This did not discourage the ELL team from migrating the Tinker and Bell mechanism to the online version in 2021. The reconstruction of the element constitutes a welcome addition to the new version, a kind of homage to the "golden age" of hypertext, and the first media translation of the mechanism in the history of hypertext reconstructions. As a narrative device it is not compulsory.

A different approach would have to be made if the Tinker and Bell keys are not a heritage feature but a fully functional narrative/navigational device. In the case of *In Small and Large Piece*s, a preservationist would need to include the functionality among the primary elements of migration. Quite likely, because of the importance of the Tinker and Bell keys for the display of navigation choices in this particular work, and especially if mobile browsers are targeted, the keyboard key combination would have to find its equivalents also on the touch interfaces, something that the Web edition of *Figurski at Findhorn on Acid* did not have to do.

Link Names and Paths

One of the popular features of early Storyspace literature's navigational system are "paths." Formed by one or more links of the same type, they helped authors semantically cluster lexias along their connections. The type of link is a custom, author-made label that – once created – could be reused to mark other links with that same label. For the reader, paths are not explicitly visible as groups but as link names on the link menu. A single item on the menu is a line describing a single available connection. On the right side of the line is the name of the destination; on the left side, the name of the connection. The latter is technically a link name, but functionally it represented a larger category of a path that grouped more than one connection. On the reader's side, the path is perceptible either as a link name in the link menu or a link label on the Storyspace map. On the writer's side, at least until Storyspace 2 (1999), paths are created and controlled from a dedicated Path Builder tool and the Path View of the structure. The Path View, accessible in some versions of the freely distributed Storyspace Reader, forms a bridge between the authorial and readerly view of the paths.

As a narrative device, paths are used in several inventive ways by authors. Joyce used paths first as a lexia management tool that would help the author and the reader orientate among the multiple narrative sequences. For example, in *afternoon, a story* the path "Lolly(call)" gathers connections related to Peter's attempt to call Lolly. This strategy mirrors the reader's attempts to progress further into the story when some of the connections to the actual conversation are restricted by guard fields.

"Lolly(later)," respectively, groups connections to lexias on the next narrative level when the attempts to talk to Lolly are succeeded. At the same time, Joyce uses paths in a playful way when some of the events or phrases are extracted from the text, commented and improvised upon to produce a path label with added meaning. Paths labeled "sweet miss terry," "sylvan ceded," "tart films" are the result of improvisational linguistic riffs on the themes encountered in the story. When read on link menus (in *afternoon, a story*) and in maps (in *Twilight, A Symphony*) these path names introduce another important layer of signification. Although mostly it is of paratextual and metafictional importance, the framing of story that paths deliver can play an important role in understanding the plot and its contexts.

In Deena Larsen's *Samplers*, paths are famously used to create a literal poetic effect in link menus. Single lines on the Storyspace link menu, with the left part labeling the path and the right the link's destination, form a poetic syntax together with neighboring lines. In effect, the link menu can be read as a poem. In *Samplers* Larsen created a whole series of poetic vignettes on link menus. It is hard to imagine a Web translation of this hypertext without the paths component because it amounted to a distinguishing feature of the work. While serving as a clear example of the "lyrical quality" of links for scholars (Bernstein 2002: 177; Tosca 1999: 217), the link menus were also strongly integrated with the theme of *Samplers*. The works' central visual motifs are colorful, interconnected quilt pieces. In this context, the lines of link menu poems not only serve as connections and lines of a poem, but also reinforce the theme of semantic, poetic nature of stitching things together

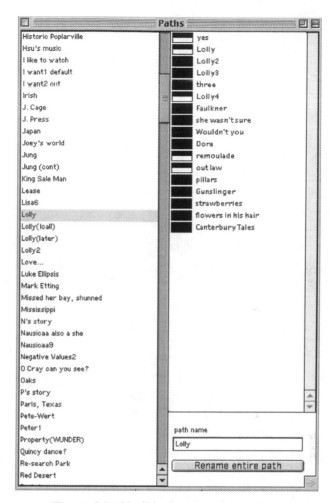

Figure 8 Pathbuilder in *afternoon, a story.*

and forming larger patterns out of the connections. Migrating *Samplers* outside of Storyspace without a translation of link menus would seriously diminish such artistic message and produce a media translation equivalent to an abbreviated version of a literary classic, made for an audience that is for one reason or another not ready, or not in need, to read the whole work.

From the narrative design point of view, paths offer an additional orientation tool for authors working with Storyspace. The tool is often an indication of grouping possibilities that found their individual implementations when authors decided to introduce their own takes on the idea of paths. Just as Holeton introduced his own Navigator that would help readers traverse storylines of *Figurski at Findhorn on Acid*, Moulthrop's vast hypertext *Victory Garden*, containing, as mentioned previously, 993 lexias, introduces its "map of the garden." Emphasizing the importance of certain nodes Moulthrop populates three parts of the garden's map with names of important lexias. Clicking on them will not only lead to a given text segment, but also initiate a narrative sequence starting at this particular point of departure. Such prominent lexias, for example "Dear Emily," "Demo," and "Thea's war," indicate narrative lines that do not necessarily align with the function of Storyspace paths. In the 2022 Edition Moulthrop relabeled these thematic hubs as "streams."[6] (Figure 9) A selection of original Storyspace paths is also migrated to this edition. They serve as a counterbalance to streams and present a more random grouping of lexias not necessarily joined by the same subject, event, or character. An index of fifty-two pages initiating paths is available for readers from the toolbar menu. Many of them correspond to the names and starting lexias of paths in the original. However, association of pages to paths is more explicit, and the content of sequence is more under control. For example, more than sixty pages are grouped along the path "Upside down." However, in the 1991 Edition, although the path starts from the same lexia "More," only one other named "8–19–91" has the path label "Upside down." The remaining fifty or more pages in 2022 Edition are the result of authorial selection from the sequence(s) of lexias that follow after "8–1991." Moulthrop explains paths in the following manner: There are fifty-two Paths through *Victory Garden*. Except for the special "Garden" path, they do not constitute linear or coherent readings, but skip around the work in devious ways. They're a bit like opening a book at random – or, in one interesting case, turning the pages backward. If you're looking for something approximating conventional fiction, stick with the "Garden" path. If exploration is your thing, try some of the others. The Pathfinder page has links to all of them (Moulthrop 2022).

Victory Garden 2022, just as the 2021 Web edition of *Figurski at Findhorn on Acid*, represents a case scenario when authors are involved in the migration and media translation of their own work. Such a situation allows for emphasis on important aspects of a specific digital poetics and for daring decisions on how to present the work to the contemporary reader. Moulthrop's focus on paths and streams, hypertext concepts with no obvious equivalents on modern reading

---

[6] For example the label "Demo" from the north part of the map of the garden leads to a lexia called "Demo" and into a sequence about a right-wing gang stealing a small tour bus and driving to Thea's house. Trouble is brewing because Thea is a vocal, progressive academic, and the gang plans to do a threatening stand-off by her house. The sequence of the stream "Demo" in *Victory Garden 2022* recounts the whole story with the confrontation and the accidental burning of the bus. The sequence in the original leads only halfway, to a point when the gang stops the bus to ask for directions to the neighborhood where Thea lives. The 2022 sequence "Demo" is longer, more exhaustive, and more focused.

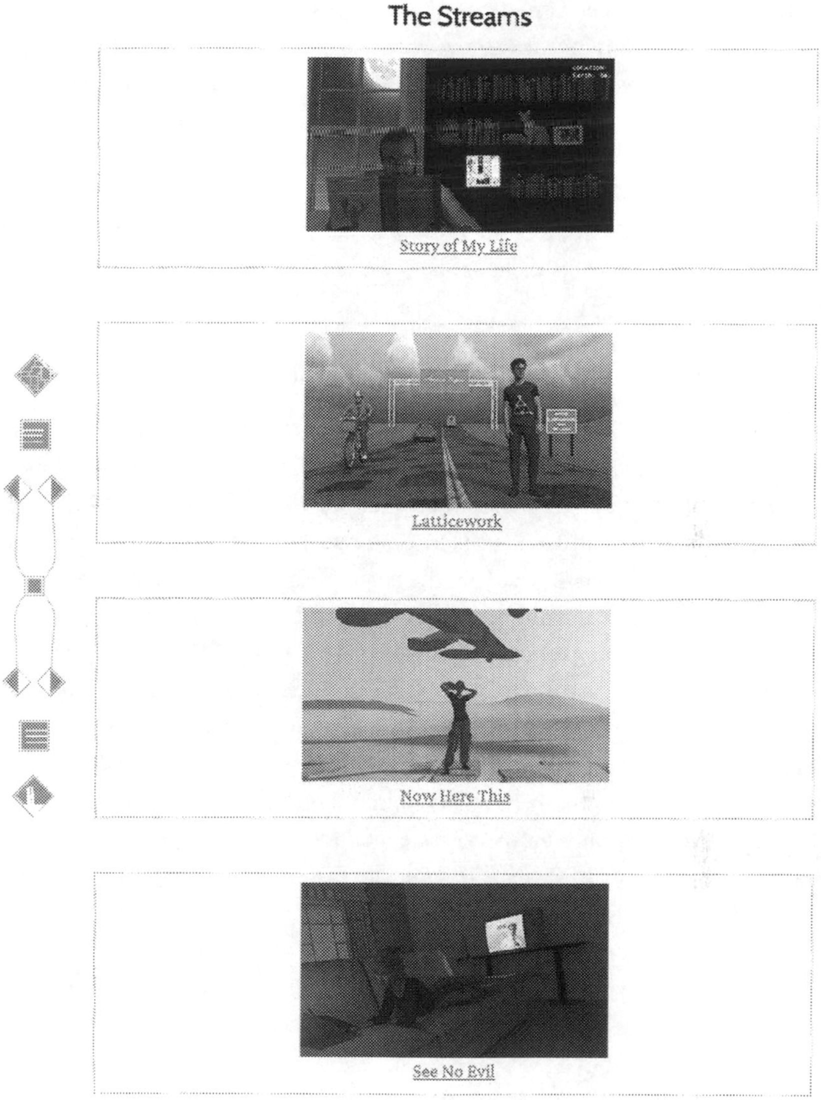

The Streams

Figure 9 Streams in *Victory Garden 2022*.

interfaces, would likely not raise the same level of attention if the project was carried out by an uninitiated preservationist or media archaeologist. The fact that the author migrates and reimagines the component of paths and that the grand narrative arc of this vast hypertext is a special path on its own, comprising forty-four streams read chronologically, as Moulthrop explains, is significant. It brings a book-like experience for new audiences and resurrects an important, although slightly exotic, component of narrative discourse of hypertexts.

Restorations and reconstructions of classic born-digital fiction give contemporary readers who might not know where to place paths – along with other exotic narrative devices – a chance to expand their digital literacy and engage in playful explorations of a text. The flexibility of the Web and its open technologies allow for various implementations of any of the classic authoring tools within the contemporary context. More and more Web reconstructions of classic stand-alone born-digital literature prove that there are numerous ways in which a media translation can be made. It bodes well for the future of this editorial and artistic practice.

Case Studies in Media Translation

The Web edition of *Figurski at Findhorn on Acid*, created by Grigar's lab with support of the author, is the first media translation of born-digital literature in which Storyspace maps are reconstructed for the Web. Each of the 354 lexias of the hypertext is visually represented on a view reminiscent of the original Storyspace Map View as a labeled rectangle connected to other lexias. The links between the rectangles of nodes are represented as strings and their directions as arrows. Moreover, maps in the Web edition of *Figurski at Findhorn on Acid* visually recreate the hierarchical structure of the hypertext by representing higher level lexias as containers for lower-level ones. Web users, just as the original Storyspace users, can click on the container with nested segments and be transferred into the lower level of the map where the view is focused only on the lexias contained within the previously visited text segment. This way, the multilayered dimension of Storyspace maps, one of their defining features, is also migrated on the Web and with it a possibility of visual navigation across the whole text. Such alternative reading practice, which allowed for a free-form exploration of the fictional universe and its representation within the space of interconnected nodes, was so far only possible in a stand-alone format of Storyspace.

The reconstruction of Storyspace maps was achieved by employing JavaScript (jQuery framework), CSS (Cascading Style Sheets), and hand-crafted drawings of rectangles and links between them (Figure 10). jQuery and CSS display the maps' content in a dedicated pop-up window, or modal, by assembling ready-made bitmapped graphics of lines, arrows and curves. The unit of representation on the map is a group of lexias on the current level of hierarchy. For example, lexias "Acid 1.x," "Spam 1.x," and "Pig 1.x" are contained within the "Artifacts" lexia. When reading about a particular artifact, a mechanical pig in "Pig 1.x" for example, readers have access to the map of the three artifact lexias. "Pig 1.x" is not highlighted as a lexia in focus, something

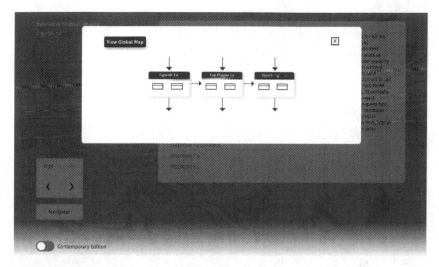

Figure 10 Map view of the Web edition of Figurski at *Findhorn on Acid.*

that would happen in Storyspace, but presented within its closest neighborhood. Readers can visually travel to further levels of the map. Inside "Pig 1.x" there are two more lexias, "Pig 2.x" and Pig 3.x," and by clicking onto the body of "Pig 1.x's" rectangle, we are transported on the layer of the map representing "Pig 2.x" and Pig 3.x." There are no further nodes inside these segments, however. In the original Storyspace version the reader could navigate their way back to the upper layers of the map by using the compass (rose wind) functionality of the main navigation bar or by pressing the enter/return key. In the Web edition readers can click on either "Pig 2.x" or "Pig 3.x" to load the new page.

Although this solution does not fully reflect the experience of the classic edition, it does bring an elegant simplification of map exploration determined by the nature of Web and page browsing and provides contemporary audiences with an understanding of the work's original functionality. Clicking on the body of the rectangle representing a lexia will bring a map of lexias it contains. Clicking on the title of the rectangle or on the body when no lower-level content exists will transport readers to the text content of the lexia. These two simple rules make the map navigation consistent and clear. To ensure that readers do not get lost in the map exploration, the lab introduced the "View Global Map" button in the top-left corner of each map modal. By activating the button, readers are moved back to the general view of the hypertext map, displaying all its parent containers. Using the browser's back button in combination with the local and Global Map view buttons, readers are never lost and can always, in a quick succession of *actemes* retrace steps either by going back to the general map of the text, or – step by step – by reversing movement one lexia at a time.

Just like the whole project, which aimed both at bringing a new, contemporary look and feel of Holeton's hypertext, and at recreating the look and feel of the stand-alone classic from two decades ago, the online maps of *Figurski at Findhorn on Acid* come in two flavors: Contemporary and Classic.

As mentioned previously, the Classic map mode is rendered in a modal that visually refers to a legacy Macintosh, specifically one running System Software 9.2. The rectangles on the map have squared corners and simple, black shadows borrowed directly from the original Storyspace map. The Contemporary map mode is shown without extra frames, in a slick, minimalist window with rounded corners. This minimalistic direction is preserved on the map itself where each lexia is drawn with rounded corners and a subtle blurred shadow. What is missing in both maps of the new Web edition is an extra-textual and visual overlay with additional information about the links connecting the elements on the maps. In Storyspace, the inbound and outbound connections to a rectangle on the map are signaled by an arrow pointing to that rectangle. Additionally, a link label, or path name, of the incoming or outgoing connection is displayed. Because maps in the Web edition of Holeton's work are assembled out of ready-made elements, and links in particular, a system of link labeling of every connection would be incompatible with the system of link drawing. What this edition gains by not migrating this aspect of the original, apart from losing a bit of the original's visual clutter, is a welcoming simplification of map usage, its refocusing on simple functionalities of seeing the current text in its context and having local and Global Map views as a constant reference and help. Getting lost in the maps of *Figurski* AD 2021 is much more unlikely than in *Figurski* AD 2001. Any minor losses during the migration process do not hinder its main achievement: While making the work finally accessible to the new audience, the major goal of preservation is achieved with an innovative, pioneering trait. Storyspace maps, deemed impossible to implement by hypertext authors in the early 1990s, finally made their way into the Web thanks to the open Web technologies.

Almost a year after the Web edition of *Figurski at Findhorn on Acid* was released, the Web edition of Joyce's *Twilight, A Symphony* introduced its own implementation of Storyspace's trademark feature: the map views. The reconstruction of Storyspace maps from the original 1996 hypertext relies on D3.js, a modern JavaScript library for data visualization on the Web, popular among media outlets for the range of tools it offers for displaying and manipulating documents based on data. In the case of any hypertext, the most important data to be visualized and manipulated is a list of links and lexias, information about the direction of links along with titles of lexias and links. The resulting map view, just as in the original, offers an alternative way of accessing the text comprising of over 300 segments of lexias, yet unlike in the Web edition of *Figurski at Findhorn on Acid*, where a noticeable degree of custom, visual reconstruction of Storyspace map view was present, the maps in the Web edition of *Twilight, A Symphony* rely much more on standard components of network visualization available within D3.js. For example, force-directed graph drawing algorithms are used in maps, shapes of nodes can be changed almost instantly, and network graphs could have many variants based on a range of available community-sourced templates and solutions.

The maps of the Web edition of Joyce's *Twilight, A Symphony* achieve two goals. While recreating some basic functionalities of their original counterparts in Storyspace, they also aim at complying with modern ways of data visualization. The resulting experience makes the two types of maps more generative, data driven, and perhaps more interactive. In the Connections Maps, for example, the visual outlook of the map depends strictly on the list of incoming and outgoing connections. As such, it breaks away from the original authorial design of maps afforded by Storyspace and offers an alternative way of presenting the same hypertext data. It can render some unexpected results. For example, a lexia, entitled "after," randomly links to all 345 nodes of the hypertext. Such a wide array of random connections would not be displayed on the original Storyspace map because it only shows links present on the current layer, and one layer usually contains no more than thirty lexias. The algorithm that executes the display in D3.js disregards the layer-based segmentation and renders all lexias of the hypertext within the map modal of the lexia "after."

The additional interactivity that the online translations of Storyspace map bring to the experience of the work comes from the force-directed graph drawing algorithm. Lexias on the map can gravitate toward each other, or be pushed away by each other, when a selected rectangle on the map is manipulated by mouse cursor or finger. This D3.js feature, popularized by modern methods of displaying nodes and links, but not present during the "golden age" of hypertext literature, supplants the new edition of the work with contemporary, technological *signi temporis*. In future editions, when new, open technologies of data visualization on the Web will replace the existing ones, some other facets of node-link representation might come to the foreground, enriching once again the life of the born-digital of literature.

Original Storyspace maps offer readers a smooth and instantaneous switch between the text view and the map view of the currently read segment. Left-clicking on the map opens its text window. Activating links in the text window instantly transfers readers to the relevant map view of a destination lexia. The speed of these transitions makes the sequence of steps necessary to swap between the two reading strategies, visual and textual, very short. The number of interaction units necessary to go from text view to map view is reduced to one: following the link/clicking the segment on the map. In the environment of the Web, the ease of such transitions is lost. Both *Figurski at Findhorn on Acid* and *Twilight, A Symphony* require readers to go from the text view to the map view of a single text segment and traverse to another segment's map view. The journey is longer, the experience is altered, yet both works – more than two decades after the original publication – achieve something remarkable: With media translation they bring back to life both the text and the essential qualities of hypertext experience and make them available again for the original audiences as well as new ones.

Restrictions of Media Translation

The migration of a fully functional, paid edition of a work of born-digital literature to a freely available Web edition never happens without a cost. Even in cases where such cost is minimal, there still remains a question of copyright, ceding of rights, and any potential benefits for the author or the publisher to maintain accessibility to the work. For example, in the case of the Polish edition of *afternoon. a story*, legal considerations made the first full migration of the Storyspace hypertext into the Web environment partially restricted. Eastgate Systems, Inc. required that the translation could not be freely available online. After paying the initial licensing fee to the company, the Polish publisher Korporacja Ha!art was committed to distributing *afternoon, a story* as a digital file for the Web browser on CD-ROM. Although the Polish edition can be read in Firefox, Opera, Internet Explorer, and Safari browsers – which makes it a cross-platform and cross-browser experience – it cannot be accessed online. In the context of long-lasting restoration and preservation of digital heritage, the offline-only limitation constituted a relatively minor hindrance. However, because the work is both offline and behind a paywall, its reach was limited from the start and destined to die out when the publisher ran out of copies of CD-ROMs. Later media translations, such as *Figurski at Findhorn on Acid*, Disch's *Amnesia*, and Joyce's *Twilight. Symphony*, are all available freely with permissions from authors and publishers, outside of any paywalls and to the widest possible audience of the Web.

Because copyright restrictions differ among countries, publishers, and specific works themselves, it is not possible to recount all regulations and the ways these regulations are applied to all works of born-digital literature. Archives held in the lab for the Electronic Literature Organization contain contracts between publishers and artists for a variety of venues, each handled differently. When restoring or reconstructing a work of born-digital literature, the lab follows the copyright rules for that specific work. In the case of the Web edition of *Figurski at Findhorn on Acid*, it was assured by the author that he did indeed receive full rights to the work. With *Amnesia*, the lab received permission from the Disch Estate to reconstruct it. Even sharing a digital version of a work published by Eastgate Systems, Inc. owned by the lab via porting it on a hard drive requires the lab to receive written permission to do so. Contrarily, all Web editions the lab produces are offered as an open-source resource through a Creative Commons Attribution Non-Commercial Share Alike license.

Concluding Thoughts on Media Translation

Numerous challenges and difficult decisions await the authors of future media translations of born-digital literature. Translators could rely on a series of migrations for a variety of competing mobile and desktop platforms; or they could rely on a single, cross-platform Web app, a solution independent of any system and accessible by any browser. The forthcoming publication of the French translation of *afternoon, a story* in Twine in production by Arnaud Regnauld, Anne-Laure Tissut, Stephane Vanderhaeghe, and Gabriel Gaudette-Tremblay might shed some new light on other possible solutions.

If, as Hans Georg Gadamer claims about translating print literary works, "reading is already translation, and translation is translation for the second time" (Gadamer, qtd Biguenet and Schulte: ix), then translating a work of born-digital literature across its various material and digital components adds the additional level of transcoding to its translation. This means that any media translation results in three levels of translation: that of the reading, that of the rendering of the source language into the target language, and that of the transformation of it from its original programming language in a new one.

While on the one hand a "translator betrays" the original work, they are, on the other hand, engaged in an act of "salvation, bringing to the translated text the kind of long life it could not possibly have in the original ... especially when the original is in an obscure language" (Keeley 54)— or, in the case of early hypertext literature, published on physical media for outmoded hardware and software.

3 Editions and Versions

It arrived by mail as a gift from a colleague. When she had previously described its cream-colored vinyl folio with maroon lettering with the graphic image of the yoni symbol, we thought immediately that it was one of the editions of

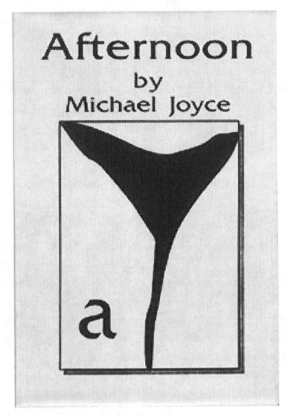

Figure 11 Folio for the 1991 Edition of *afternoon, a story.*

Michael Joyce's *afternoon, a story* missing from the lab's library and from the archives of The NEXT: the 1990 Edition also known as the 1st Eastgate Imprint–certainly a rare find (Figure 11). Two other editions we were missing are even rarer: the editions of the work published in 1987 and 1989 by Riverrun Ltd. that Joyce distributed at conferences and shared with colleagues. Joyce reported that only fifty copies of the former and twenty-seven of the latter had been produced, a handful only extant in private collections and the Michael Joyce Collection at Harry Ransom Humanities Center. A year before, we had examined all the editions held in the lab, all published by Eastgate Systems, Inc. from 1992 to 2016, and studied the scholarship about the three missing ones. Without the ability to travel to study The Michael Joyce Papers during the pandemic, we had to rely heavily on what Matthew Kirschenbaum, Terry Harpold, and others had reported about these earlier three editions. Eagerly slipping the floppy disk into drive of the Macintosh Classic II, we were delighted that the work, now thirty-two years old, launched. Excitement shifted to surprise when the feature reportedly in the 1990 Edition – the double loading screen – was not present. Also perplexing was the information conveyed on the title screen: that this work was in fact an "Eastgate Press 2nd Edition" published in 1991, copyrighted in "1987, 91" – an edition and publication date we did not know existed and not reported in any scholarship about this hypertext novel.

What we can deduce from examining this work is that two editions, one in 1990 and another in 1991, were published by Eastgate Systems, Inc. and packaged in the same folio design. The 1990 would be the first edition of the work Eastgate Systems, Inc. published, replete with the double loading screens originally found in the two editions Joyce had published himself, but by 1991 the publisher had been able to unite the two loading screens into one and, then, republished the work that same year, calling it its 2nd Edition. This discovery meant the work to identify editions and versions of *afternoon: a story* we had labored on so hard now needed amending. It also made us wonder how many more exist that we do not know about? Of course, a bigger question may be why does it matter?

afternoon, a story: A Study of Editions and Versions

Since its introduction in 1987, *afternoon: a story* has appeared on six different media formats, first on floppy disk from 1987 to 1994, on the Web in 1997, as an excerpt in a print book in 1998, on CD-ROM in 2001 and 2007, and on USB Stick and downloadable digital file in 2016. Additionally, it has been translated into four languages, including Italian (1993), German (1998), Polish (2015), and French (2018). So popular is the novel that an unofficial emulated version of the 1990 Edition running on Mini vMac has been circulating for years. A study undertaken by Lyle Skains shows that it is the most cited of all hypertexts published by Eastgate Systems, Inc., far-stripping even Shelley Jackson's *Patchwork Girl* – 55,280 citations of Joyce's as opposed to 2,830 for Jackson (Skains 2022).[7] It would not be a hyperbole to say that few other works of early hypertext literature have seen so much effort in maintaining its accessibility to the reading public than *afternoon: a story*. An in-depth study of *afternoon: a story's* media formats over its history shows that variations in the work occurred with each migration to a new format. As such, the work makes an excellent case study for the importance of establishing editions and versions of born-digital literature and using this specific information about a work when referencing them in scholarship. In many cases, changes to the work's code affecting its functionality and interface design are sometimes so significant that

---

[7] The presentation was given as part of "Legends, Myths and Magic of Electronic Literature Full Day Open House Workshop," chaired by Grigar for ELO 2022 in the session called "Women in E-Lit."

when we read criticism of the work, we are compelled to ask, "Which *afternoon* is the author referring to?"

As mentioned in the section on media translation, the most defining feature of born-digital literature is its code. Tied inextricably to its underlying software as it is, *afternoon, a story*, therefore, exists in two realms: as "programmable media" (Cayley, qtd. in Rettberg 2019: 3) and as literature. We can also point to Manovich's model and say that it consists of two distinct layers: the computer layer and the cultural layer (2002: 46). The term attributed to its genre – that is, hypertext novel – recognizes this duality and points to a "resistan[ce] to clear lines of demarcation" (Rettberg 2019: 9). This hybrid state as computational literature, comprising computer and cultural levels at the same time, lends itself to an organization strategy built on both "versions" and "editions."

Versioning, Kirchenbaum says, is "a hallmark of electronic textual culture" (2008: 197). Grounded in John Bryant's work, *The Fluid Text: A Theory of Revision and Editing for Book and Screen*, Kirchenbaum lays out an early account of the versions of *afternoon, a story* in his book *Mechanisms: New Media and the Forensic Imagination*. As he says:

> Versions may be either physical (literally distinct documents) or inferred from the evidence available on one or more extant documents; a version of a work can always be linked to another version; versions are revisions of the works, and they may be initiated, either deliberately or inadvertently, by the author or by some other agency like an editor–or the public at large; versions do not depend on the authority of the author to be authorized as a version; versions are manifest by their degree of difference from other versions. (2008: 187–188)

For a work like *afternoon, a story*, which experienced so many changes to its software – Storyspace, as well as Macintosh System Software, MacOS, and Windows – over its lifetime, it is important to differentiate the specific *afternoon, a story* to which we are referring when talking about the work.

The concept of an edition developed out of the print world and has been, heretofore, the way in which *afternoon, a story* has often been discussed (Kirschenbaum 2002: 27) – a convention we follow in this Element. In terms of editions, we borrow Fredson Bowers' notion devised for hand-printed books, defining it as "the whole number of copies of [the work produced] at any time or times from substantially the same [approach]" (1994: 39), rethinking it for our needs in terms of its underlying code, language, and presentation. There may be many copies made from any one edition over a length of time, but a new edition is identified as the work released again with changes to presentation, structure, and/or text. An edition is not reliant upon changes to a work's code that results in a new version, but every new version *does* result in a new edition. This means that when *afternoon, a story* was published in the book *Postmodern American Fiction: A Norton Anthology*, it became the 11th Edition of the work but did not register as a new version. On the other hand, when Norton published it the year before on the Web, the work became the 10th Edition and Version 9.0.

Finally, by "text" we mean "language that is ... doing some job in some context, as opposed to isolated words or sentences that ... might put on the blackboard" (Halliday and Hasan 1985: 10). They are, as David M. Levy suggests, "bits of the material world ... that we create to speak for us and take on jobs for us" (2000: 25). Ultimately, text is a "social process" (Dahlström 2002: 140) that can potentially weave together, as Hayles argues, numerous "signifying components" including "sound, animation, motion, video, kines-thetic involvement, and software functionality, among others" (2002: 20). In sum, decisions made about versions and editions take into account a broad notion of what constitutes the work that we know as *afternoon, a story*.

As the discovery of the heretofore unknown 1991 Edition of *afternoon: a story* shows, the process of versioning and identifying an edition is challenging but extremely necessary for scholars who wish to know how best to access a work or discuss it with some level of exactitude. For example, it can be read on a Macintosh Classic II sold from 1991 and 1993 and running System Software 6.0.7 and is even compatible with the Macintosh SE sold from 1987 to 1990 and running System Software 6.0.3, but it does not launch on the Macintosh Performa 5215CD sold from 1995 to 1996 and running System Software 7.6 – but the 1992 Macintosh Edition does.

While preparing for the thirtieth anniversary of the commercial release of *afternoon, a story*, an event entitled "An Afternoon with *afternoon*,"[8] a history of the novel's publication was produced and made accessible to the audience. That history has now been updated to include all translations of the novel and the additional new version published in 1991. Finding accurate information for editions is a difficult task. Eastgate Systems, Inc. did not make a habit of dating the folios of the works it published, and its website does not list the publication dates nor maintains a publishing history of the works it released. One can check the "Created" and "Modified" dates of any of the early works published for Macintoshes by clicking the Option + i keys. But without access to the floppy disk, such as the problem we faced with the 1987, 1989, and 1990 editions of *afternoon, a story*, we need to look elsewhere for assistance.

---

[8] See the event website at https://dtc-wsuv.org/afternoon-with-afternoon/index.html.

Scholarly databases are not always a reliable resource for electronic works. WorldCat, for example, does not always distinguish floppy disks from CD-ROMs. Publication dates for the same version may differ. It lists the 3rd Edition Eastgate floppy disk, what Kirchenbaum calls the "authoritative" edition of the work (2002: 31) as having been published in 1992 *and* 1993. The CD-ROM is listed as having been published only in 2001, though it was republished in 2007 for computers running MacOS X 10.5 and later. One of its listings for a floppy disk version displays art for the CD-ROM's insert instead of the art used for the floppy disk. The publisher's website offers an excellent description of the novel, along with reviews and basic bibliographical information but, as mentioned previously, does not list all of the editions and versions of the work released over time – only the current offering published on a USB Stick and the downloadable digital file.

This means that to produce a useful publication history of *afternoon, a story*, we must rely on two main sources: First, copies of works on hand in the lab's library and the archives belonging to the Electronic Literature Organization held and managed by the lab; and, second, from information about the three missing editions found in the scholarship published by those who have had the opportunity to experience those editions. Thus, this study relies heavily on Belinda Barnett's excellent chapter, "Machine-Enhanced (Re)Minding: The Development of Storyspace," from *Memory Machines: The Evolution of Hypertext*; Matthew Kirschenbaum's insightful essay "Editing the Interface: Textual Studies and First Generation Electronic Objects" and *Mechanisms: New Media and the Forensic Imagination*; and Terry Harpold's *Ex-foliations: Reading Machines and the Upgrade Path*. Additionally, Harpold's excellent bibliography from that book has informed our general approach to numbering the editions. Conversations with Joyce, Harpold, Bernstein, and Moulthrop, and Grigar's own memories stemming from her first contact with *afternoon, a story* as a graduate student studying under noted hypertext scholar Nancy Kaplan also contribute greatly to this history.

The numbering system developed for *afternoon, a story* builds on the system reported in Harpold's book as well as the colophon of Norton's *Postmodern American Fiction's* special Web edition. Like Harpold, Grigar counts the 1992 edition for Windows computers but also includes the one from 1994. *Postmodern American Fiction* makes no distinction between the Macintosh and Windows editions in its numbering system, but Grigar does. She also follows Harpold's lead relating to the 2001 date of the CD-ROM and adds the later edition. Finally, she includes the release of the USB Stick and download-able file edition that came after the publication of the anthology and Harpold's book. In total, eighteen editions and fifteen versions of *afternoon, a story*, dating from 1987 to 2016, have been published, world-wide.

The 1987 Edition and the 1989 Edition – "The Riverrun Editions". 1st (1987) and 2nd (1989) Editions; Versions 1.0–2.0

The first two editions of Michael Joyce's *afternoon, a story* are produced with an early iteration of Storyspace developed by Riverrun, Ltd., the company founded by Jay David Bolter, John B. Smith, and Joyce. The software is written in PASCAL (Kirschenbaum 2008: 188) and realized at the time only for the Macintosh environment, the creators' platform of choice (Barnett 2014: 123). While Kirschenbaum refers to these two editions as "beta" editions (2002: 27), Joyce himself considers them to be "finished literary work" (Barnett 2014: 129).

The 1987 Edition is recognized as the 1st Edition of the work (2008: 181). According to Joyce, approximately fifty copies were distributed on the floppy disk format to participants at the 1987 ACM Hypertext conference at the University of North Carolina at Chapel Hill by Jay David Bolter and himself (Kirschenbaum 2008: 32). Kirschenbaum points out the anomaly found in this edition of the node, "Jung," "that contains no inbound links and no scripted text," an issue corrected in subsequent editions (2008: 32). It was read on a Macintosh computer, Plus or greater, with a floppy disk drive and 160K RAM.

The 2nd Edition released in 1989 is a revision of the 1st Edition before its publication the following year by Eastgate Systems, Inc. Joyce said he distributed copies of this edition to participants at the Second ACM Conference on Hypertext, November 1989, held in Pittsburgh, PA, believing only a total of twenty-seven copies had been produced (Joyce 1992a). Kirschenbaum, who conducted in-depth research of *afternoon, a story* at the Harry Ransom Center where Joyce's papers are held, expands upon this information, adding that it was "distributed to some subscribers to IF, *The Journal of Interactive Fiction* and *Creative Hypertext* (edited by Gordon Howell); and a few copies were also distributed at Hypertext '89" (2008: 160). The difference between the 2nd Edition and 1st Edition, according to Kirschenbaum, is that the 2nd "took advantage of certain changes to Storyspace to add new links and create a few new places" (2002: 29).

The 1990 Edition – "The 1st Eastgate Imprint": 3rd Edition; Version 3.0

After Bernstein of Eastgate Systems, Inc. licensed Storyspace from Riverrun, Ltd. on December 17, 1990 (Barnett 2014: 134), he rewrote the software in C, renumbering it as Storyspace 1.0 (2008: 189). Bernstein is credited for "pioneer[ing] hypertext publishing . . . and arguably legitimiz[ing]hypertext as

for directions click yes (y)-- to start press Return
©1987,92 Michael Joyce
Eastgate Press 3rd Edition 1992   12345...
PO Box 1307
Cambridge, MA 02238

Figure 12 Landing screen of the 1990 Edition of *afternoon, a story.*

a creative endeavor" (Barnett 2014: 132). The work is listed on the title page as "'afternoon' in Readingspace," "Version 2.0d format" and copyrighted 1985–1989.

The 1990 Edition, referred to by Joyce as the "1st Eastgate Edition," was published on floppy disk with Storyspace for Macintosh computers and packaged in a cream and maroon vinyl folio (Figure 12). The front cover of the folio shows the name of the work with the yoni, the Hindu symbol of the womb. The symbol is also used for the launcher icon, thus emphasizing the novel's exploration of women and their relationships with men (Grigar 2016). The back cover features the famous line: "I want to say that I may have seen my son die this morning," as well as a description that highlights the work's literariness: "Michael Joyce's *Afternoon* is a pioneering work of literature, a serious exploration of a new hypertextual medium. It is neither a game nor a puzzle." A testimonial by hypertext author and theorist Moulthrop follows. Contained within the folio, along with the 3.5-inch floppy disk, is a booklet that features a license agreement, warranty, and disclaimer, as well as critics' testimonials and the author's bio. Thus, the presentation of the work and the work itself bridge the worlds of electronic and print media and signal that the former is a serious, intellectual endeavor. This graphic is found in the title screens of all but two editions that follow.

Kirschenbaum reports that the 1990 Edition "changed text windows and typefaces and made minor fixes of links and texts, all differing from the [previous] edition" (2002: 29). Readers familiar with the later editions of *afternoon, a story* and other Storyspace hypertexts will notice that in this edition the loading screen, which came to represent a work's size and hypertextual complexity, is divided into two: one for the spaces and another for the links – 539 and 950, respectively. Without access to the previous two editions, it is not possible to know if this variation of the loading screen is a holdover from the Riverrun Editions or if Eastgate Systems, Inc. introduced the two screens for its own imprint. In any case, they are consolidated into one screen in the next edition. It is also important to note on the start page of the work that the copyright reads "©1987 Michael Joyce" and "The Eastgate Press Edition 1990."

To access this edition of *afternoon, a story* readers need a Macintosh computer 512E or above with a floppy disk drive. The 512E was released by Apple on April 14, 1986, and at the time cost $2,000.

The 1991 Edition – "The Single Loader Edition": 4th Edition; Version 4.0

As stated at the beginning of this section, the discovery of an edition published in 1991 was surprising in light of the fact it had never previously been mentioned in scholarship relating to the novel. It may have been easy to overlook considering that it is packaged in the same cream vinyl folio as the 1990 Edition. Additionally, readers may not have paid attention to the shift from the double loading screen used in the previous edition to a single loading screen found in this one since they may not have been aware of the previous approach or were completely new to the hypertext environment and not aware of such specificity. Besides the single loading screen that shows up in all of the subsequent editions and versions of the work for Macintosh computers published on floppy disk, it is also copyrighted "1987, 91" and features Pamela McCorduck's recommendation published in *The Whole Earth Review* from spring 1991 on the title page. This new edition shows the speed at which innovations were taking place at Eastgate Systems, Inc. to streamline the software and the growing reputation of the novel in the literary world.

The 1992 Macintosh Edition and the 1992 Windows Edition – "The Authoritative Editions": 5th and 6th Editions; Versions 5.0–6.0

The 1992 Macintosh Edition, packaged in a gray and blue folio instead of the cream and maroon colors of the previous edition, is a release that addresses the upgrade to Macintosh Systems Software 6.0.7. As mentioned earlier, it has been referred to as the "authoritative text of *afternoon, a story*" (Kirschenbaum 2002: 31). Readers will note, however, that its title screen identifies it as the "3rd Edition." The discrepancy in the publisher's edition number can be explained by studying the title screens of the editions published on the CD-ROM and USB Stick: Both show that the publisher acknowledges the copyright dates of 1987 and 1992 but disregards the 1989 and 1991 Editions. Additionally, Harpold refers to the 1992 Macintosh Edition as the 5th, citing the 1992 Windows 3.1 Edition as the 4th (2009: 316) since he did not know of the 1991 Edition and followed a strategy whereby he often numbered the Windows edition of the work ahead of the Macintosh. It is clear, however, from examining copies of *afternoon, a story* that a Macintosh edition was created and released before a Windows edition. In fact, this was a practice followed by Eastgate Systems, Inc. for all its titles.

By the time the 1992 Edition was released, the novel had received rave reviews by Robert Coover in *The New York Review of Books*, and J Yellowlees Douglas had completed her dissertation on the novel. Thus, its growing popularity resulted in a change of the back cover: Joining the previous information from the 1991 Edition are excerpts from reviews by both McCorduck and Coover and an excerpt from Douglas' essay from *Writing on the Edge*.

Besides changes to its physical presentation, the work also underwent textual and structural ones affecting its code. Kirschenbaum reports a slight increase of nodes, from 536 to 539, and large increase of links, from 854 to 951 though the copies of this edition and version used for this study register only 950 links. In all, the work grew, according to Kirschenbaum, "from 235 kilobytes in the first edition to 375 in this one due to "changes in the underlying software code and the way in which it has been compiled." More importantly, however, a revision to the linking structure "yield[ed] access to a remote region of *afternoon, a story* that opens up important new plot developments." As he points out, "this area of the text would not have been previously accessible without a far more prolonged and circuitous reading of *afternoon*" (2002: 30–31).

In terms of the software, System Software 6.0.7 was released on October 16, 1990, a mere day after 6.0.6. It was available for a wide range of Macintosh computers, including the SE, SE/30, Classic, II, IIx, IIcx, IIci, IIfx, IIsi, and LC. At the time of its release, the novel sold for $19.95, or $36.50 in today's dollars.

The Windows 3.1 Edition constitutes the first release of *afternoon, a story* for computers running Windows. Kirschenbaum references it as the 5th Edition (2008: 160), but, as mentioned previously, Harpold identifies it as the 4th (2009: 190). It is clear, however, that it was released *after* the Macintosh version had already been distributed because the manual for the 1992 Macintosh Edition makes no mention of a Windows version, nor does it include instructions for installing one.

Additionally, a flyer, entitled "Storyspace serious hypertext" and packaged in the folio for Moulthrop's *Victory Garden* (1991), advertises "More Titles" offered by the company, listing *afternoon, a story* among the eight. Below that section is another one, entitled "New! For Windows!" that includes four titles. The first work mentioned is *afternoon, a story*. The information states that it requires Windows 3.1, 386/486 and a hard drive.

The 1993 Edition – "The 1993 Italian Print Edition": 7th Edition

The 1993 Edition is a linguistic translation of the novel by Walter Vannini and Alearda Pandolfi into Italian. It appeared in the print booklet that accompanied two floppy disks containing the "first inter(net)view with Michael Joyce and the first hypernovel by an Italian author, *RA-DIO* by Lorenzo Miglioli" by Castelvecchi Editore and Vannini's own company, Human Systems, in the first volume in a series, entitled "Elettrolibri" (Vannini 2020). Fourteen years later the print translation was migrated to the Storyspace platform and republished along with the 1998 German Translation and the 2007 Edition on CD-ROM.

The 1994 Macintosh Edition and the 1994 Windows Edition – "The Final Floppy Disk Editions": 8th and 9th Editions, Versions 7.0–8.0

Because the vinyl used previously for Eastgate Systems, Inc.'s folios was found to damage its contents, when the publisher rereleased *afternoon, a story* in 1994, it shifted to cardboard as its packaging material, a practice it also undertook for the release of all of its titles published on floppy disk. Interestingly, although two different colors are used for the folios – white and blue – color is not associated with a particular platform. To determine if the floppy disk contained in the folio is compatible with a Macintosh or Windows computer, readers would need to check the folio's back cover and see if a sticker is affixed to the dot marking it "Windows" or "Macintosh."

It is interesting to note that the white folio shows the "A" in *afternoon, a story* capitalized, while it is not on the blue folio. When asked about this anomaly, Joyce said he does not know why it happened since his intention was for the title to be represented uncapitalized (2016). One hypothesis that cannot be verified is that the white folios were used first for the Macintosh Edition, but when the Windows 3.1 Edition was released, the company released both editions packaged in a blue folio with the letter "A" corrected on both the front and back covers. What *can* be verified is that the continued critical acclaim of the work impacts the design of the folio cover: It changes from the conceptual design that included the yoni symbol used for the previous two versions to one featuring a photo of the author. The back cover is also affected by the novel's growing popularity. On the white folio the author's photo is featured four times down along the left-hand side. Interestingly, this treatment is eliminated on the blue folio. On both, however, the famous line from the novel, description, and excerpt from Coover's review remain from the 1992 Editions, but replacing the other critical responses are Richard Grant's for *The Washington Post Book World*, Harry Goldstein's for *The Utne Reader*, and those from the Toronto *Globe and Mail* and the *Wall Street Journal*. Like the previous versions, the folio contains a manual – though now expanded to fourteen pages to accommodate directions for both Macintosh and Windows computers. The folio also contains a self-addressed Registration Card.

The 1994 Macintosh Edition makes no changes to the text of the work; however, its software was updated to accommodate Macintosh System Software 6.0.7 and above. Readers, however, would not notice much difference between it and the previous edition.

There are two main differences between the Macintosh and Windows versions of *afternoon, a story*: functionality and aesthetic. In regard to the former, readers using a Windows computer encounter a work framed by two bars that recall a software environment (Figure 13). The top bar includes seven menu items: "File," "Edit," "Storyspace," "Navigate," "Bookmark" "Windows," and "Help"; the bottom, items generally associated with Windows systems: "Start," "A:\," "C:\WINDOWS\Start Menu," the name of the file, which in this case is "Afternoon a story," and the time of day. The Macintosh version, on the

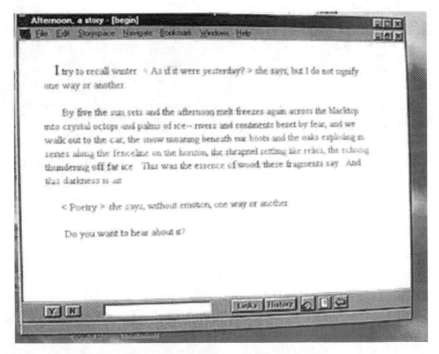

Figure 13 Interface of the Windows Edition of *afternoon, a story.*

other hand, long offered what looks more like a page of a book with a small bit of space at the top-left-hand side of the screen showing the Apple icon and the word "Reader." Interestingly, the difference in aesthetic is impacted by the difference in functionality: The Toolbar, a feature of Storyspace hypertexts from the beginning, is reorganized into the menu of the Windows version. For example, to locate the paths in a given lexia – an activity the Toolbar is used for in the Macintosh Edition – readers need to go to "Storyspace" in the menu. For many readers who came to Storyspace hypertexts before Eastgate Systems, Inc. began publishing Windows versions, the experience of reading literary hypertexts on a PC can be jarring.

It is also important to point out that the copyright date for the 1994 Macintosh Edition is listed as "1987/1992," while the 1994 Windows Edition shows "1987/1993," which further suggests that the Macintosh Edition was published before the Windows Edition.

The 1997 Web Edition and the 1998 Print Edition – "The Norton Editions": 10th and 11th Editions, Version 9.0

With Joyce's permission and help, W. W. Norton & Co. published *afternoon, a story*, along with J Yellowlees Douglas' "I Have Said Nothing, as a Web-based hypertext in 1997 and as an excerpt in its *Postmodern American Fiction: A Norton Anthology*. While making the work accessible on the World Wide Web made sense in light of the growing popularity of the platform, the emergence of a print edition surprised critics and fans of the work. Joyce himself called it "ironic" (Grigar 2016). Kirschenbaum emphasizes this oddity by italicizing the word "print" when talking about this edition (2002: 28). Some believed that the inclusion of hypertext literature in a Norton anthology and hosted on the Web by the company meant it had been recognized as a formal literary form by the purveyors of print (Grigar 2018).

The 1997 Web edition was programmed in Java and JavaScript-enabled browsers with access to LiveConnect and ActiveX support, both Windows products. Compatible browsers included Netscape Navigator 3.x for Windows 95, NT, and UNIX; Navigator 4.x for Windows 95, NT, MacOS, and UNIX; and Internet Explorer 3.x and 4.x for Windows 95 and NT; and possibly Internet Explorer 4.x for Macintosh System Software and other browsers. It offered a mere 25 of the original 528 nodes, an approach that Joyce resisted (Joyce 2022). The website credits Justin Edelson for the "Java programming and Javascript (*sic*) guard field engine"; Jason Lucas as the graphic designer; Jay David Bolter as the programmer who produced the data structure and special textual coding; and Heather Malin as the editorial assistant.

The site also references the dates for *afternoon, a story* as 1987, 1992, and 1990. While this edition still *appears* to be online at both its original URL and a secure URL, those wishing to read it, unfortunately, cannot get beyond the interface. This loss of access occurred around 2013 when main browsers stopped supporting the applets needed to run Java.[9]

The 1998 print edition is an excerpt of the novel comprising ten lexias published on pages 577–580 in the anthology edited by Paula Geyh, Fred G. Leebron, and Andrew Levy. It appears in the section entitled "Technoculture," which focuses on "technology as a "social and creative force." In the introduction to the section, the editors describe hypertext fiction as a "full partnership of computer and authorship," suggesting a "paradigm shift, linking the act of creativity with the telecommunications machines that now facilitate – and mediate – human contact" (1998: 509).

Joining *afternoon, a story* are six lexias from Douglas' "I Have Said Nothing," mentioned previously; reprints of William Gibson's short story "The Gernsback Continuum," Ursula Le Guin's "Shrödinger's Cat," and other stories; and excerpts from novels, such as Don DeLillo's *White Noise* and Neal Stephenson's *Snow Crash*. Some lexias from Joyce's story include commentary about the possible paths readers can take in the digital version, thus tying this edition with the 1997 Web edition. The date of *afternoon, a story* referenced is 1990, which speaks not to the edition of the work from which the print edition comes but rather to the one of the two copyright dates frequently used for the novel. The anthology also includes an essay about *afternoon, a story*, entitled "Conclusions," by Harpold in the anthology's last section, "A Casebook of Postmodern Theory." In his essay Harpold refers to the novel as "unruly" (1998: 638), a term echoed by Kirschenbaum (2008: 161). Because Harpold cites 539 lexias in his essay, it is clear he is talking about the 1992 Editions of the work, even though the publication date showing up in "Figure 2" of his essay gives the date 1990.

1998 – "The 1998 German Translation": 12th Edition

This is a linguistic translation into German created by Doris Köhler and Rolf D. Krause and bundled with the 1993 Italian Edition and the 2007 Edition.

Krause reports that the translation came about following a seminar taught in the summer 1996 by Doris Köhler, entitled "Digital Narration: Hypertext and Literature," at Hamburg University. Köhler was a trained computer scientist who specialized in multimedia and Apple computers, and Krause was working

---

[9] The URLs to the archival links are: (1) original URL www.wwnorton.com/college/english/pmaf/ hypertext/aft/) and (2) secure URL https://wwnorton.com/college/english/pmaf/hypertext/aft/).

on his PhD in German Lit. He was also interested in American literature and involved in developing the IT infrastructure for his department (Krause 2020b). So they came to the task of translation with knowledge of literature and computers.

It was clear to both scholars that the time devoted to *afternoon, a story* was insufficient, so an additional seminar followed that led to the idea that they translate the novel. They used a copy of the 1992 Macintosh Edition as their source text. Contact with Joyce resulted in an introduction to Vannini, the Italian translator of the work who provided them much guidance about the challenges that awaited them. A visit by Joyce in January 1997 resulted in the two-day workshop "Happy Birthday, Afternoon! Zehn Jahre Hyperfiction – und was nun?" [Ten Years of Hyperfiction – and what now?]. Krause reports that Joyce's visit provided the translators the opportunity to gain insights into the novel. He also reports that having the artist on hand injected "the poet's feeling for the sound and cadence of language.... . Looking for the right word and phrase wasn't just a lexical exercise" (2020b).

While the ten students participating in the workshop collaborated on the translation, the bulk of the labor fell to Köhler and Krause. Krause reports that a lack of time to devote to the project contributed to the years it took to complete it (2020b). Adding also to the delay was the fact that in 1999 Köhler took a position in Bremen and then a job in industry. He also remembers the technical problems the pair had with Storyspace's built-in space limitations and the fact that German translations are "always about 10 percent longer than its English original." Specifically, they were constrained by the twenty-four-character limitation for the title of a space and the lack of a scroll bar for navigating text longer than the allowable length. They also faced, what he calls, the "usual translators' problems, e.g. with words or phrases of double/multiple meaning – a flower like 'baby's breath' does not literally translate into German; in spite of their biological identity, their names have a completely different context of associations in English and German." He admits that some of the challenges were "self-inflicted" due to the project's workflow relating to managing a team of students (Krause 2020c).

The pair, however, continued to labor on through 2001, completing a draft that same year. In January 2002 they presented Joyce with a final copy when they saw him in Berlin. Three years passed before they heard from Joyce that Eastgate Systems, Inc. was planning to release *afternoon, a story*, again, on CD-ROM and that it would include both the Italian and German translations. When the edition came out in 2007, Köhler and Krause were not notified (Krause 2020a).

Because this edition was built on the same system that the 2007 Edition used, it does not constitute a new version. An important difference could be found in the order of lexias on the default reading path. The 2007 German Edition does not allow readers to progress from the "staghorn and starthistle" lexias. Instead of going to "fenceline" then "relic," then "can I help you" to arrive at the crucial juncture in the story, the lexia "I call Lolly," it diverts to "the essence of wood" then to "nuncio" and then back to "I want to say," the beginning of the default narrative sequence. We do not see this change in the edition as affecting the version number since it seems to be unintentional.

The 2001 Edition and the 2007 Edition – "The CD-ROM Editions": 13th and 14th Editions, Versions 10.0–11.0

It had been seven years since the company had released a new edition of *afternoon, a story*. When it finally did, the work came packaged as a CD-ROM in a plastic jewel case. Gone are the bookish vinyl and cardboard folios filled with promotional brochures and a booklet providing directions for how to install the work. By the early twenty-first century, the reading public had years to become inculcated by Web culture, and Joyce's audience did not need to believe they were interacting with a book to be enticed to read his novel.

The novel's art changed, too. The insert cover features a black-and-white drawing of woods, an image inspired by the scene near the publisher's office. The CD-ROM does not have a label, so its silver surface is printed with the graphic in black along with publication information. The launcher icon, which is titled "afternoon CD," opens to a VISE installer. The graphic of the woods appears on the installation screen, which simply states "Eastgate Systems, Inc." and "Michael Joyce afternoon, a story." Following its installation, a folder containing the launcher icon with the yoni symbol found in the previous versions, a manual created as an Acrobat document, entitled "Reading _afternoon, a story," and a free coupon appears. Both the Title and Start Screens are the same as those featured in the 1992 Macintosh and Windows Editions (5th and 6th Editions). This means that though released in 2001, the 13th Edition is said to be the "3rd Edition 1992." A look at the file date reveals that it is listed as Macintosh System Software 6.0.7.

The need to migrate *afternoon, a story* from the 3.5-inch floppy disk format was predicated not by aesthetics, but rather by technology: The elimination of the floppy disk drive from Apple computers beginning 1998. Eastgate Systems, Inc. had already begun to publish new titles, like Rob Swigart's *Downtime* and M. D. Coverley's *Califia*, straight to CD-ROM in 2000 and was, by 1997, releasing titles, like Stephanie Strickland's *True North* and Bill Bly's *We Descend*, simultaneously on both 3.5-inch floppy disk and CD-ROM formats. What *is* clear by looking at this version of the CD-ROM is that it functions as a breadcrumb leading readers from the conventions put into place by the company for its floppy disks in the early to mid 1990s. The bitmapped graphics and information found on its screen, as well as the need to double-click on the hyperlinks, give way to a gradual update to its interface and overall reader experience. The 2001 Edition was created with Storyspace 2.0 for computers running Windows 95, 98, NT, 2000, and ME or Macintosh computers running System Software 7.0–9.0 and early MacOS X running the Classic operating system. So, the listing of 6.0.7 in the disk information is obviously carried over from the previous version.

The need for another edition of *afternoon, a story* came about when it was clear that Apple was planning to drop its support for the Classic operating system in 2007 with the upgrade to Mac OS X 10.5 (Leopard). The 2001 Edition, like all the previous editions before it, would render this touchstone of early hypertext literature obsolete.

Strangely, information about the release of the 2007 Edition published on CD-ROM is hard to come by. Scholarly databases, ELMCIP.net and WorldCat, do not differentiate between the two CD-ROM editions, nor does the Electronic Literature Directory mention it in its entry for the novel. Using the Internet Archive's Wayback Machine to examine the publisher's Web page at the time when the work was promoted and sold shows that Eastgate System, Inc. also makes no mention at all about the release of a new edition. Even when the company updated its website in July 2009, it did not change the information on the page for Joyce's novel. Harpold, however, lists it in his bibliography, and Krause makes it clear that his translation was slated to be released after 2005. Grigar herself owns both CD-ROM editions in her library but had not paid attention to the variations between them nor pieced together their history until she began work on versioning the novel in 2020.

It seems from looking at the 2007 Edition's file date that Eastgate Systems, Inc. began work on it in 2006. It was produced with Storyspace 2.5.1 for both Macintosh and Windows computers and packaged in the same style as the 2001 Edition, which further complicates its identification as a new edition. As mentioned previously, both the Italian translation by Vannini from 1993 and the German translation by Köhler and Krause from 1998 are packaged with it, though oddly Köhler's and Krause's names are listed only by their initials. The insert cover and the CD-ROM label are similar to the 2001 Edition except that the CD-ROM is given a white label. The launcher icon is changed from the yoni to the Storyspace logo. The title screen lists this edition as the "6th" and dates it "2007." The CD-ROM's jewel case insert has not been updated and, so, still states that the "[p]ackaging, art, and documentation are copyrighted in 2001."

It is important to reiterate that the look and feel of the later editions – the 2007 Editions onward – differ from those produced on floppy disks and the 2001

Edition. The typeface used for the 2007 Edition, for example, is more up-to-date and cleaner, having lost the traditional jaggy bitmapped look. In essence, this edition set the style for future editions of the work.

The 2011 Polish Edition – "The Polish Translation": 15th Edition, Version 12.0

We go into much detail later in our multimedia book about the challenges Pisarski, Nowakowski, Jakub Jagiełło, and Łukasz Podgórni faced when migrating *popołudnie. pewna historia (afternoon, a story)* into a new software environment of Web browser technologies.

Unlike the translations into Italian and German that required no changes to the code in order to realize their editions, the Polish translation includes diacritical marks not supported by Storyspace software. The Macintosh operating systems were also not in widespread use by the Polish audience at the time of the translation. The result was a new edition and version of the work produced for the Web. *popołudnie. pewna historia* was published as an offline browser application distributed on a CD-ROM and published by Korporacja Ha!art in Kraków in 2011. The application was coded in XML and JavaScript and used xslt stylesheets to render the XML in a Web browser. The system of guard fields and conditional links was manually transposed from Storyspace link creation panels into JavaScript conditional markup. The data about the history of reading was stored in the browser's cache and handled by JavaScript functions. The launch of the application was handled by the HTML Application script (HTA). Another important feature of the original – displaying names of destination lexias in the link menu panels – was made possible thanks to some additional parsing using Python.

popołudnie. pewna historia is supported by Firefox, Opera, and Safari for both Windows and Apple computers, included with the CD-ROM. Upon its launch, a file called "przeczytaj mnie" ("let's read me") opened the start page of Joyce's classic hypertext. The disk was packaged in a thin, plastic jewel case typically used for distributing CD-ROMs and DVDs. On the cover of the insert was a black-and-white rasterized photograph of a road in a forested urban area made by Pisarski in reference to the cover of two previous editions published on CD-ROM. The publication cost 27 PLN, equivalent to $9.

The 2016 Stick Edition – "The USB Stick Edition": 16th Edition, Version 13.0

The 2016 Edition of *afternoon, a story* was released in the same year optical disks were discontinued on Macintosh computers. It had been nine years since the 2007 Edition had been published and five years since Apple's introduction of MacOS X 10.7.5. When it arrived in the hands of readers, it was packaged as a USB Stick. As of this writing, it is only compatible with Macintosh computers. It is important to note that only three works from the forty-eight published by Eastgate Systems, Inc. have been released in this media format: *afternoon, a story*, Shelley Jackson's *Patchwork Girl* (1995), and Bernstein's *Those Trojan Girls* (2016).

A comparison between the editions Eastgate Systems, Inc. published on floppy disk with those published from the 2007 Edition onward shows a marked difference in aesthetic, with the latter three editions (2007, 2016 USB Stick, 2016 Downloadable Digital File) offering a contemporary interface that readers of the early twenty-first century had come to expect from interactive media. While the 2007 Edition still displays testimonials on the back insert of its jewel case extolling the work as a hypertext, neither the 2016 Stick Edition nor the 2016 Downloadable Digital File Edition includes no such information. As with all editions of *afternoon, a story*, the work opens to a title page. This one is, however, identical to the 2007 Edition, identifying it also as the "6th Edition 2007" with the two copyright dates, "1987, 1992," also mentioned. Because screen resolution had continued to improve over the ensuing years, the title page is larger than with the previous edition, leaving more white space on the right-hand side of the screen and further deemphasizing the logo and associated information. The typeface, though, remains the same as the 2007 Edition. It should be noted, though, that the graphic featured on the title page is the same one used for previous editions except when accessing the work with a computer running MacOS X 10.15.5 (Catalina). Readers with computers running this operating system will also notice the opening graphic is missing. Also of interest is that the graphic used for promoting the 2016 Stick Edition on Eastgate Systems, Inc.'s website is the cover art from the editions published on CD-ROM – that is, the black-and-white image of the woods. By moving away from an aesthetic introduced in the 1990s, though, the 2016 Edition continues to resituate the work for a contemporary audience begun with the 2007 Edition.

The 2016 Downloadable Edition – "The Downloadable Digital File Edition": 17th Edition, Version 14.0

The 2016 Downloadable Digital File Edition of *afternoon, a story* is a significant departure from all others. As a downloadable digital file, it lacks the physicality of the previous sixteen editions presented on various media formats – floppy disk, CD-ROM, and even the USB Stick of the 16th Edition that the novel closely resembles in aesthetic and functionality. Unlike the 1998

Web edition, the only other edition that was not packaged on a physical media format, the 2016 Downloadable Digital File Edition comes to readers as a Dropbox link to a .dmg file, a format commonly used for moving apps to a computing device. Like the 2016 Stick Edition, it provides none of the contextual materials connecting it to literature or past editions, like quotes from Coover and other critics, promotion as a "postmodern classic," an author bio, the image of Joyce on the cover, a cover graphic, and so on. The edition exists outside of the system of referents with which it had long been associated as a novel – hypertext or otherwise.

A hint of this shift occurred over a decade before when the 2007 Edition of *afternoon, a story*, changed the launcher icon from the yoni symbol to the Storyspace software logo. Even at the time it seemed odd for the novel to lose this connection to its past, but since Eastgate Systems, Inc. had taken this step with all works it had migrated to Storyspace 2.0 and published on CD-ROM, there was consistency in the decision. Looking back, it serves as a harbinger for other technological changes shaping the public's relationship with electronic media. Just a year before, in 2006, cloud technology became mainstreamed with Amazon through its Web services. Users were becoming accustomed to downloading media from sites and interacting with files instead of handling physical objects, like floppy disks and CD-ROMs that had been used traditionally by Eastgate Systems, Inc. for its publications. By the time the 2016 Stick Edition appeared, the public had been reading novels off a Kindle for well over a decade and via the Apple iBook app for six. An electronic novel like Joyce's was no longer expected to look like a print book, much less possess the physicality of one. It could, in fact, exist simply as a file.

2018 – "The French Edition": The 18th Edition, Version 15.0

In 2013 a team of translators led by Arnaud Regnauld started to work on the French translation of *afternoon, a story*. Until 2018, the main reference available for the team, apart from the 2001 Edition published on CD-ROM owned by Regnauld, was the 1998 Web edition, published by Norton. Having translated the text, but with no prospects of publishing the translation within the original Storyspace environment, the team decided to call its project a "virtual translation" (Vanderhaeghe 2013) and reflect on translatological and philosophical potential of the act of migrating the "spectral body" of the text from one language, and medium, to another (Regnauld 2013). From 2018, with the arrival of Gabriel Tremblay-Gaudette, the team has been preparing the migration of the work onto the Twine platform (Tremblay-Gaudette 2021), which is at the time of this writing forthcoming.

The Big So What?

A study of the many editions and versions of *afternoon, a story* over its three-decade lifetime tells us much about the work itself and the technological and cultural changes that have taken place over time.

First, the way in which the presentation of *afternoon, a story* transformed from a book-like folio replete with many of the conventions of a serious work of print fiction (e.g., endorsements by reviewers, cover photo of the author) to a downloadable file from a cloud service speaks to a cultural transformation where literature is no longer confined to print and novels can take the form of electronic media. From its beginning born-digital literature had been described by scholars like Bolter as "electronic," as a form of book or writing (1991: 3). The floppy disks and later CD-ROMs were necessary for storing the work and porting it to a computer for access. Works like McDaid's *Uncle Buddy's Phantom Funhouse* that incorporated other physical media into the narrative were rare. Thus, the shift today to accessing *afternoon, a story* via cloud technology brings the work close to its electronic roots.

Second, it is clear that scholars working in the field of born-digital literature need to designate the edition of a work with which they are working because, in the case of *afternoon, a story*, differences occur between editions published on floppy disk and among those published on other formats. As mentioned earlier, the number of links reported by Kirschenbaum for the 1992 Edition differs from the 1990 Edition. Using the latter as the source text for translating the work would result in a potentially different work than a translation that used the former. Moreover, scholars working with an edition published on floppy disk for Windows computers would certainly experience the novel differently than those reading it on a Macintosh computer. Specificity is important and should be the norm for rigorous critical writing about born-digital literature.

Finally, such a study demonstrates the challenges of keeping born-digital literature accessible, and it highlights the important role digital preservation and conservation play in maintaining our cultural and literary history. In this regard, *afternoon, a story* serves as a cautionary tale. Maintained in no less than eighteen editions and made accessible on six different formats over its thirty-one-year history – withstanding along the way the technological upgrades to both hardware and software and the growing popularity of streaming media – speaks to its legacy and the impact this work has had on contemporary literary culture. It also speaks to the evolution of hypermedia over time: the loss of physicality of the object, the move away from features and attributes associated with book and print culture, and the changing nature of publishing in the Digital Age.

[1] Kirschenbaum reports 951 links but the copies Grigar has in her lab show 950. We are not clear about why there is a discrepancy between the numbers.

[2] Some other translators might decide that for them the most authoritative edition, or version, is the one that they are able to access at the time of translation. For example, in 2001 this could be the Windows version of *afternoon, a story* with the radically redefined interface. If the translator decided that they want to pursue the Windows version as the main point of reference, the experience of the translation would be quite different.

4 Restoration and Reconstruction: Final Thoughts

Naked. Alone in a hotel room. No memory of how you got here much less who you are. The room contents – an Apple IIe, a Gideon Bible, room key, ballpoint pen, stationery – provide no immediate clues to help you. You are on your own to solve the mystery of your identity.

This is the conceit of Disch's *Amnesia*, the interactive game published by Electronic Arts (EA) in 1986. The manuscript Disch produced for the game is well over 400 pages in length and involves players escaping the Sunderland Hotel (and perhaps a shotgun wedding) to potentially 4,000 locations and 650 streets in Manhattan. Episodes take place in an electronics store, Washington Square Park, the New York Historical Museum, the Chelsea Hotel, and a posh loft in Soho, among others, until players learn who they are. At least ten endings are possible: A sheep

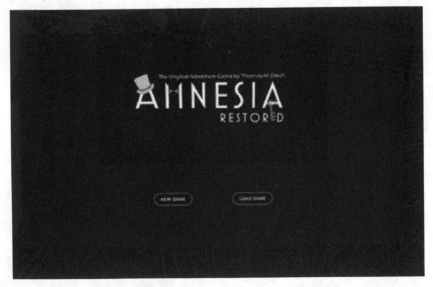

Figure 14 Interface for *Amnesia Restored*.

farmer in Australia? At the river Styx with Charon? Death by firing squad? Helping players to navigate, virtually, one of the largest cities in the world are three physical items packaged with the two 5.25-inch floppy disks: the "A Visitors Guide to New York City" (that also doubles as the Sunderland's information piece for its customers), the "Street and Subway Map of Manhattan," and the" X-Street Indexer" that gives cross streets for all avenues. Intended originally for the Apple IIe and then migrated to the Commodore 64 and IBM PC, *Amnesia* with its strong novelistic approach was not commercially successful as a game, but it developed cult status among fans for its innovative approach to digital storytelling and quirky storyline.

Reconstructing a game for a contemporary audience who, over the thirty-five years since its original publication, had come to expect full-color graphics, more interactivity, and intuitive gameplay was but one of the challenges that awaited the lab's preservation team. It was also tasked with restoring large swaths of the story EA had omitted but the author wanted to see in the game. There also remained the problem of integrating the physical media needed to solve the mystery into the game's mechanics so that the experience of consulting them to play the game would be a seamless experience for the player.

The new edition, called *Amnesia Restored*, required reading the 400+-page manuscript provided to the lab by Bernstein and Sarah Smith, studying Disch's notes that provided insights into the portions of the story Disch wanted restored to the game, figuring out a strategy for restoring the omitted parts into the game mechanics, reviewing sketches and plans Disch (or someone working with him) left behind, mapping the streets of Manhattan where the game's action takes place, and playing the game over and over again on the Apple IIe in the lab and via the emulated version available for download – all before writing one line of code.

One Size Does Not Fit All

As *Amnesia* demonstrates, preserving born-digital literature requires a variety of activities driven by the specific needs of the object itself (Figure 15). What the preservation team needed to do to make *Amnesia* – produced originally in a programming language called FORTH – accessible differed widely from the activities undertaken for Coverley"s "Fibonacci's Daughter," created with HTML; John Zuern's digital poem, "Ask Me for the Moon," produced with Flash; or Deena Larsen's series of seventeen short poems, "Kanji-Kus," created with iFrames and Java Applets; Annie Grosshans' hypertext essay, "The World Is Not Done Yet," originally built in Adobe Muse; or Holeton's *Figurski at Findhorn on Acid*, produced on the Storyspace platform. One size does not fit all; each calls for its own unique approach to conservation.

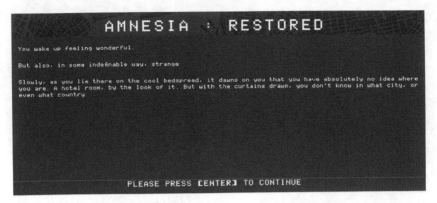

Figure 15 Landing page for *Amnesia Restored*.

It is also apparent when preserving born-digital literature that there exists a continuum of interventions needed to make works accessible again. As a work produced originally for the Web, Coverley's "Fibonacci's Daughter" needed little intervention except to convert the MIDI files into MP3 files and recode the website to reflect this change. The demise of Flash in December 2020 meant that the lab needed to implement Ruffle to Zuern's "Ask Me for the Moon," which involved simply adding the requisite few lines of code to the page hosting the work's SWF file. In both cases, the new versions were checked against the originals on legacy computers that still support the original software to ensure integrity of the media translation.

Some endeavors entail more time and resources. Larsen's "Kanji-Kus" required the lab to migrate some of the work's HTML files and all of the art and text into a new Web environment; replace the image maps created with Java Applets into JavaScript; and recode the parts of the work to eliminate the iFrames. To ensure the integrity of the media translation, the reconstructed version was checked against the original on a legacy computer in the lab that still displays iFrames and reads Java Applets. On the other hand, the original media and text of Grosshans' essay were migrated, but the work was completely reprogrammed to eliminate the thousands of lines of erroneous code that Muse added needlessly to the work. Checking the new version against the original on a legacy computer made it possible for the lab to adjust the timing of the text animations so that they unfolded at the same tempo as the original. Holeton's novel presented a unique problem for the lab: As a beloved classic Storyspace hypertext, it needed to retain some of the characteristics of that platform and, at the same time, be reconstructed as an open archival version for the Web. The lab's team migrated the text, remade images so that they fit the resolution of contemporary computers, and, as mentioned previously, developed two interfaces to reflect two different reading modes – one with a full-color interface for a new audience *and* another that reflects the reading experience of the original on an Macintosh computer running System Software 9.2 – which at the time of the novel's release would have been what the audience used to access the work. This double reading strategy allows readers to toggle back and forth between these two modes as they experience the work. Multiple reading modes were also created by the lab's team for *Amnesia* so that players can experience the game on a contemporary interface, as well as on the interfaces for the Apple IIe, Commodore 64, and IBM PC.

The continuum of interventions, therefore, constitutes three major activities that may involve preservation methods – emulation, migration, and/or collection – in varying degrees and result in new versions and, thus, editions of a work: Restoration and Reconstruction. We call the intervention into *portions* of the code (including changing linking structure) and/or aspects of the functionality of a work to make the work accessible again "restoration." Such efforts entail low-level media translation. We call the *complete* rebuild of a work that affects its code and may also impact its functionality and presentation "reconstruction." Such efforts entail mid- to high-level media translation. Thus, digital preservation in these contexts involves unique conservation practices identified for the specific needs of a particular work.

Restoration projects undertaken by the lab's team include, as mentioned, Coverley's "Fibonacci's Daughter" but also the hundreds of Flash works restored via Ruffle for The NEXT. Besides Disch's *Amnesia*, Larsen's "Kanji Kus," Grosshan's "The World Is Not Done Yet," and Holeton's *Figurski at Findhorn on Acid*, the lab reconstructed Smith's *King of Space* built on the Hypergate platform, an early hypertext authoring system reminiscent of HyperCard, and published on two 3.5-inch disks; and Moulthrop's hypertext novel, *Victory Garden* and David Kolb's philosophical essay, "Caged Texts," both produced with Storyspace.

For Smith's *King of Space* the lab consulted with the author and her two manuscripts and notes and played the game on a legacy computer – a Macintosh PowerPC G3 – that still reads the game's floppy disks. The preservation team made several videos documenting their gameplay that could be used to guide their plans and development. Because the team did not have access to the original code and the intent was to make an archival version of the game for contemporary computers, they built the game from scratch in HTML, CSS, and JavaScript, capturing the work's functionality through their gameplay and observations. While the 314 lexias of text were migrated from the original edition, *King of Space*'s narrative was streamlined to follow one major path of the story to provide coherency. Along with a complete overhaul of the code, major changes were also made to the game's interface and presentation (Figure 16). Full-color images, animations, and 3D models, for example, were created and inserted into appropriate places in the story. A soundtrack was composed for the game, and music and sound added to the work. The mini-games, which in the original version often resulted in players getting stuck and needing to restart the game, were revamped and made more intuitive. In sum, this reconstruction project reflects a massive undertaking that took a team of twenty-six programmers, designers, animators, composers, and content specialists – and the input of the artist – over five months to complete.

On the other hand, Moulthrop's *Victory Garden* was reconstructed by a small team of eight, which included the author, who migrated the work from Storyspace into Tinderbox and then outputted into HTML and CSS. The hypertext structure was rebuilt so that the reading experience follows along forty-five "Streams" (or what amounts to episodes) or by multilinearly via "Paths." Like other reconstruction projects, *Victory Garden 2022*, as it is called, resulted in an update to the interface (Figure 17). A vertical pervasive menu takes the place of the original horizontal Toolbar, and full-color images produced by the artist are used throughout. The background color of the interface, however, harkens back to the neutral color scheme of the original, and the logo retains the iconic "labyrinth" to provide some consistency across editions.

Kolb's "Caged Texts," named after John Cage and the most experimental of the texts Kolb wrote for *Socrates in the Labyrinth*, was never published. In devising it, Kolb, a philosopher, consulted texts in his personal library, opening each one at random and entering a portion of that page as lexia to a node in

Figure 16 Landing page for the Web edition of *King of Space*.

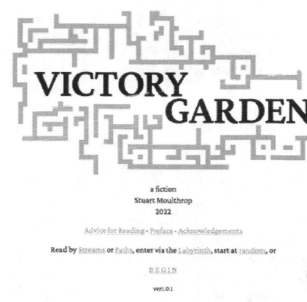

Figure 17 *Victory Garden 2022* landing page.

Storyspace, which, when read, would appear randomly. Because it was produced in Storyspace, it could, like *Victory Garden*, be exported to Tinderbox and outputted to HTML files.

This part of the work was undertaken by Bill Bly, the author of *We Descend* who also published on the Storyspace platform. Bly tested the original in different versions of Storyspace (vv 2.51b1 through 3.90) and Tinderbox (vv 4.7.1 through 9.1.0b542) to get the proper result. He also ensured the work's linking structure – the default text links – was successfully migrated and tagged the guard fields and loops for building the navigation. Because the outputted version was simply a series of HTML files, the lab was required to build a version of the work that not only included CSS but also a responsive design. The hyperlinking structure was built with JavaScript and channeled Cage's experimental approach to art by allowing the various lexias to appear randomly. Likewise, the team randomized the interface to further represent Cage's experimental approach to art.

Joyce's *afternoon, a story* was created as the first work for Storyspace, and this way served as a test environment both for the software itself and for the whole genre of hypertext fiction. As mentioned in the previous section, it was reconstructed in 2011 by the preservation team in Poland led by Pisarski, with the plan for it to be accessible in the offline mode of Web browsers. The reconstruction coincided with the development of the Polish translation of

Joyce's work, and, as such, this reconstruction of the work is only available in the Polish language. The work was rebuilt in XML, CSS, JavaScript, and with some scripting in Python. Each lexia of text is an .xml document rendered in the browser through the xslt stylesheets. The system of guard fields and conditional links was manually transposed from Storyspace link creation panels into the JavaScript conditional markup. The history of reading is stored in the browser's cache, and the launch of the Web application is handled by the HTML Application script (HTA). To recreate the classic OS system error sound, the preservation team programmed a stop sound, or system error sound, when the default reading ended that prompts readers to choose links from the menu. This new version was distributed and sold on a CD-ROM inside a slim DVD case holder. The front cover of the case had an original graphic inspired by the 2001 CD-ROM edition of *afternoon, a story*.

The same team reconstructed Joyce's *Twilight, A Symphony* in 2015 in Polish and again in 2022 in English. The hypertext novel was, like *afternoon, a story*, created with Storyspace. Published in 1996, it was Joyce's first multimedia hypertext fiction, with more than thirty illustrations, sound snippets (of field recordings, songs, and a short lullaby sung by the author), and even a video clip. Multimedia components were accompanied by a free-form visual navigation of the hypertext structure via the Storyspace Map View, a feature not available in Joyce's *afternoon. a story*. The 2015 reconstruction utilized the same reconstruction framework as the Polish version of *afternoon. a story* but migrated fully to the Web (the offline only requirement made by Eastgate, Systems, Inc. was by that time lifted). All illustrations and a selection of sound files, as well the video file, were extracted from the original and placed on the Web. The 2022 reconstruction of *Twilight, A Symphony* constitutes an entirely new version. The code was rebuilt in HTML, CSS, and JavaScript from a modified Storyspace 2 export and from the "link report" file sent by Eastgate Systems, Inc. The guard field system and link menus were recreated in JavaScript, while visual navigation on Storyspace maps was recreated with the use of the D3.js JavaScript Framework. Container lexias on the map are clickable and lead to lower layers of the hypertext structure. An extra map view "Connections Maps" is available. Its functionally resembles the Storyspace Roadmap View that presents connections to and from the current lexia. Screenshots of original illustrations were updated with the use of AI photo enhancement tools. Over thirty sound files containing Joyce's readings of selected lexias are available from the navigation toolbar.

In sum, the restoration and reconstruction projects presented in this section required, in varying degrees, approaches like migration, emulation, and collection as part of the digital preservation process. In some cases, text and images were migrated while code was completely rebuilt. Other cases saw a bit of code added to a HTML page to update a file name. Still in other cases, no migration or emulation was required, but a slight change in the code predicated the need to check the new version against the original on legacy computers. What this means, then, is that preservation approaches – emulation, migration, collection – serve larger purposes in the work we do – restoration and reconstruction – and are applied in specific and unique ways to conserve both the integrity of a work and its ongoing accessibility.

The current state of born-digital literature is always a precarious one endangered not only by technological innovation but also by corporate interests – both of which often outstrip concerns for maintaining cultural heritage. Those of us who remember Steve Jobs' complaint that Flash was out of step with "low power devices, touch interfaces, and open Web standards" (Salter and Murray 2014: 136) saw it as a potential rallying cry for Adobe to develop a suitable solution for maintaining the thousands of works of art produced with the software. Instead, the company gave up on Wallaby, the program it launched in 2012 for converting FLA files to HTML5, and issued a series of emergency patches to stave off malware until the company completely stopped supporting it in 2020.

As we have shown, it is possible to restore and reconstruct early born-digital works, but the labor and resources it takes to do so can be cost-prohibitive and time-intensive. On the other hand, not engaging with this activity means a substantial loss of intellectual history of the early twenty-first century. As Abby Smith Rumsey points out, though contemporary society is "being drowned in the data deluge," it is important to recognize that "human learning, a shared body of knowledge and know-how to which each of us contributes and from which each of us draws sustenance … is the creation of multiple generations across vastly different cultures" (2016: 12–13). The poignant question she poses is, "What can we afford to lose?" (2016: 7). Is it, we ask, Moulthrop's *Victory Garden*, which grapples with a war in Kuwait at a time when Americans were still reeling over the political turmoil wrought by a war in Viet Nam? Or Smith's *King of Space*, which highlights the power of women in a genre long dominated by male heroic adventures? We contend that all of the early born-digital works discussed in this Element contribute both to an understanding of the cultural concerns reflected in these works *and* to the larger notion of human expression as it developed during the early decades of the digital age.

We have argued throughout this Element that works of born-digital literature are not immaterial, yet it does not make them less ephemeral. From the vantage point of ancient culture, the fate of Sappho's poems in particular, dependent as they were upon material objects to sustain and preserve the artistic expression, is equally futile. We may console ourselves that unlike the constraints of writing technologies and storage practices that left us with a mere 15 percent of the lines of Sappho's poetry, the digital files of Larsen's reconstructed "Kanji-Kus" – so easily copied and distributed – have a better chance of survival. Predictions for the long-term endurability of HTML are hopeful. But what of the works produced with proprietary software? We may be comforted that *Uncle Buddy's Phantom Funhouse* lives on as an emulation at the Internet Archive or an unauthorized emulated edition of *afternoon, a story* on Mini vMac is being circulated by friends, but these attempts to preserve works via emulation, as we have argued, distance the reader from the physicality of the original work and so are mere band-aids on the larger problem of maintaining their integrity. What we need in order to fulfill the dream of a world that values our cultural history is the recognition that the born-digital literature we are losing is, first, worth saving, and, second, requires attention *now* while the physical media and hardware are still available to digital preservationists and the artists and publishers who produced them are still among us to guide preservation activities that ensure integrity. In that vein, we offer this Element as a call to action.

References

Primary

Coverley, M. D. (2000) "Fibonacci's Daughter." *New River: Journal of Digital Writing and Art*, 7. www.cddc.vt.edu/journals/newriver/coverley/Fibonacci/f2.htm.

(2021) "Fibonacci's Daughter (Version 2.0)." *The NEXT*. https://the-next.eliterature.org/works/1064/0/0/.

Cramer, Kathryn (1994) *In Small & Large Pieces*. 3.5-inch floppy disk for Macintosh. Watertown, MA: Eastgate Systems.

Disch, Thomas M. (1986) *Amnesia*. Two 5.25-inch floppy disks for Apple IIe. Redwood City, CA: Electronic Arts.

(2020) "The World Is Not Done Yet, Version 2.0" *Electronic Literature Collection Volume 4*. https://collection.eliterature.org/4/theworldisnotdoneyet.

(2021) *Amnesia Restored (Amnesia, Version 2.0)*. https://amnesia-restored.org.

Grosshans, Annie (2013) "The World Is Not Done Yet." Self-published.

Holeton, Richard (2001) *Figurski at Findhorn on Acid (Version 3.3, The Canonical Edition) CD-\ ROM for Macintosh and Windows*. Watertown, MA: Eastgate Systems.

(2021) Figurski at Findhorn on Acid (The Web ed.). *The NEXT*. https://the-next.eliterature.org/works/1102/0/0/.

Joyce, Michael (1987) *afternoon, a story*. The 1987 ed. 3.5-inch floppy disk. Riverrun.

(1989) *afternoon, a story*. The 1989 ed. 3.5-inch floppy disk. Riverrun.

(1990) *afternoon, a story*. The 1990 ed. 3.5-inch floppy disk. Watertown, MA: Eastgate Systems.

(1991) *afternoon, a story*. The 1991 ed. 3.5-inch floppy disk. Watertown, MA: Eastgate Systems.

(1992a) *afternoon, a story*. The 1992 Macintosh ed. 3.5-inch floppy disk. Watertown, MA: Eastgate Systems.

(1992b) *afternoon, a story*. The 1992 Windows 3.1 ed. 3.5-inch floppy disk. Watertown, MA: Eastgate Systems.

(1993) *afternoon, a story*. The Italian ed. 3.5-inch floppy disk. Trans. Walter Vannini in Lorenzo Miglioni (ed.), "Elettrolibri." Milan: Human Systems.

(1994a) *afternoon, a story*. The 1994 Macintosh ed. 3.5-inch floppy disk. Watertown, MA: Eastgate Systems.

(1994b) *afternoon, a story*. The 1994 Windows 3.1 ed. Watertown, MA: Eastgate Systems.

(1996) *Twilight, A Symphony*. CD-ROM for Macintosh. Watertown, MA: Eastgate Systems.

(1997) *afternoon, a story*. The 1997 Norton Web ed. *Postmodern American Fiction: A Norton Anthology*. New York: W. W. Norton.

(1998) *afternoon, a story*. The 1998 Norton Print ed. *Postmodern American Fiction: A Norton Anthology*. New York: W. W. Norton.

(2001) *afternoon, a story*. The 2001 CD-ROM ed. Watertown, MA: Eastgate Systems.

(2007) *afternoon, a story*. The 2007 CD-ROM ed. Watertown, MA: Eastgate Systems.

(2011) *afternoon, a story*. The 2011 Polish ed. Trans. Radosław Nowakowski, Mariusz Pisarski and Jakub Jagiełło. Kraków: Ha!art.

(2015) Twilight, A Symphony, Web. Trans. Radosław Nowakowski, Mariusz Pisarski, and Jakub Jagiełło. Kraków: Ha!art.

(2016a) *afternoon, a story*. The 2016 USB Stick ed. Watertown, MA: Eastgate Systems.

(2016b) *afternoon, a story*. The 2016 Downloadable Digital File ed. Watertown, MA: Eastgate Systems.

(2018) *afternoon, a story*. The French ed (unfinished). Trans. Arnaud Regnauld, Anne-Laure Tissut, Stephane Vanderhaeghe, and Gabriel Gaudette-Tremblay.

(2022) *Twilight, A Symphony*. Web. Trans. M. Pisarski and M. Furgał. London: Techsty.

Kendall, Robert (1996) *A Life Set for Two*. CD-ROM for Macintosh and Windows. Watertown, MA: Eastgate Systems.

(2000) "Penetration." Web. Watertown, MA: Eastgate Systems, www.eastgate.com/Penetration/Welcome.html.

Kolb, David (1997) "Caged Texts." Digital file. Unpublished.

(2022) "Caged Texts." Web. *The NEXT*. Forthcoming.

Larsen, Deena (1999–2002) "Kanji-Kus." Self-published.

(1993) *Marble Springs 1.0*. 3.5-inch floppy disk for Macintosh. Watertown, MA: Eastgate Systems.

(1997) *Samplers: Nine Vicious Little Hypertexts*. CD-ROM for Macintosh. Watertown, MA: Eastgate Systems.

(2020) "Kanji-Kus." http://dtc-wsuv.org/wp/ell/deena-larsens-kanji-kus/.

Malloy, Judy (1993) *Its Name Was Penelope* (The Eastgate ed.). 3.5-inch floppy disk for Macintosh. Watertown, MA: Eastgate Systems.

(1995) Uncle Roger. *The WELL*. Web ed.https://people.well.com/user/jmalloy/uncleroger/partytop.html.

(2016) *Its Name Was Penelope* (The Scholar's Version). DOSBox. Watertown, MA: Eastgate Systems.

McDaid, John (1992) *Uncle Buddy's Phantom Funhouse*. Five 3.5-inch floppy disks for Macintosh. Watertown, MA: Eastgate Systems.

Moulthrop, Stuart (1989) *Hyperbola: A Digital Companion to Gravity's Rainbow*. Self-published.

(1991) *Victory Garden* (The Eastgate ed, Version 5.0). 3.5-inch floppy disk for Macintosh. Watertown, MA: Eastgate Systems.

Moulthrop, Stuart (1992) *Dreamtime*. Self-published.

(2022) Victory Garden 2022. Web. *The NEXT*, https://the-next.eliterature .org/works/1999/0/0/.

Nelson, Jason (2013) "Nothing You Have Done Deserves Such Praise." *Turbulence*.

(2021) "Nothing You Have Done Deserves Such Praise, Version 2.0" *The NEXT*. https://the-next.eliterature.org/works/946/0/0/.

Secondary

Aarseth, Espen (1997) *Cybertexts: Perspectives on Ergodic Literature*. Baltimore, MD: The Johns Hopkins Press.

Adobe. "Adobe Fonts" (n.a.) https://fonts.adobe.com/fonts/cotton.

Auslander, Philip (2008) *Liveness: Performance in Mediatized Culture*. New York: Routledge Books.

Balcerzan, Edward (1998) "W Stronę Genologii Multimedialnej," *Teksty Drugie* 6(59): 7–24.

Barad, Karen (2003) "Posthumanist Performativity: Toward an Understanding of How Matter Comes to Matter," *Signs: Journal of Women in Culture and Society* 28(3): 801–831.

Barnett, Belinda (2014) "Machine-Enhanced (Re)Minding: The Development of Storyspace," in Belinda Barnett (ed.), *Memory Machines: The Evolution of Hypertext*. London: Anthem Press, 115–136.

Bernstein, Mark (2002) "Storyspace 1." *Proceedings of the Thirteenth ACM Conference on Hypertext and hypermedia*, 172–181.

(2016) "Storyspace 3." *Proceedings of the 27th ACM Conference on Hypertext and Social Media*, 201–206. New York: ACM.

Biguenet, John and Rainer Schulte (1989) *The Craft of Translation*. Chicago, IL: The University of Chicago Press.

Bogost, Ian (2012) *Alien Phenomenology, or, What It's Like to be a Thing*. Minneapolis: The University of Minnesota Press.

Bolter, Jay David (1991) *Writing Space: The Computer, Hypertext, and the History of Writing*. Hillsdale, NJ: Lawrence Erlbaum Associates.

Bolter, Jay David and Richard Grusin (1999) *Remediation: Understanding New Media*. Cambridge, MA: The MIT Press.

Bouchardon, Serge and Bruno Bachimont (2009) "Preservation of Digital Literary Works: Another Model of Memory?" www.utc.fr/~bouchard/wp-content/uploads/2009/12/2009-05bouchardon-bachimont-epoetry09.pdf.

Bowers, Fredson (1994) *Principles of Bibliographical Description*. Princeton, NJ: Princeton University Press.

Bryant, John (2002) *The Fluid Text: A Theory of Revision and Editing for Book and Screen*. Ann Arbor, MI: Michigan University Press.

Butterfield, Andrew, Gerard Ekembe Ngondi, and Anne Kerr (2016) *A Dictionary of Computer Science*. Oxford: Oxford University Press.

Coover, Robert (1992) "The End of Books." *The New York Review of Books*. June 21. https://archive.nytimes.com/, www.nytimes.com/books/98/09/27/specials/coover-end.html.

Dahlstrom, Mats (2002) "When Is a Webtext?" *Text Technology: The Journal of Computer Text Processing* 11(1): 139–161.

Dolphijn, Rick and Iris van der Tuin (2012) *New Materialism: Interviews & Cartographies*. London: Open Humanities Press.

Douglas, Jane Yellowlees (1994) "Are We Reading Yet? A Few Suggestions for Navigation" [Author's Introduction to the Web Excerpt of:] *I have Said Nothing*, https://wwnorton.com/college/english/pmaf/hypertext/ihsn/i_have_said_nothing.html.

Ensslin, Astrid (2007) *Canonizing Hypertext: Explorations and Constructions*. New York: Continuum.

(2019). "'Who Shattered the Looking Glass?' A Critical Essay about Kathryn Cramer's 'In Small & Large Pieces'," in Dene Grigar, Nicholas Schiller, Holly Slocum et al. (eds.), *Rebooting Electronic Literature: Documenting Pre-Web Born Digital Media, Volume 2*. Vancouver: Nouspace Publications. https://scalar.usc.edu/works/rebooting-electronicliterature-volume-2/index.

(2022) *Pre-Web Digital Publishing and the Lore of Electronic Literature*. Cambridge: Cambridge University Press.

Fludernik, Monika (2001) "New Wine in Old Bottles? Voice, Focalization, and New Writing," *New Literary History* 32(3): 619–638.

Gadamer, Hans Georg (1975) "To What Extent Does Language Prescribe Thinking?" *Truth and Method*. Trans. Garrett Braden and John Cumming. London: Sheed and Ward.

Galloway, Alexander R. (2012) *The Interface Effect*. Cambridge: Polity Press.

Gärdenfors, Peter (2003) *How Homo became Sapiens: On the Evolution of Thinking*. Oxford: Oxford University Press.

Geyh, Paula, Fred G. Leeborn, and Andrew Levy (1997) *Postmodern American Fiction: A Norton Anthology*. New York: W. W Norton.

Goldstein, Harry (1994) "Review of *afternoon, a story.*" *Utne Reader*. March–April, 131–132.

Grant, Richard (1993) "Never the Same Text Twice." *Washington Post Book World*, July 11, 8–9.

Grigar, Dene. (2002) "Mutability, Medium, and Character." *Computers and the Humanities* 36: 359–378.

(2016) "Ten Things I Learned about *afternoon, a story.*" May 4. http://dtc-wsuv.org/wp/pathfinders/2016/05/04/10-things-i-learned-about-afternoon-a-story/.

(2018) "Saying Something about 'I Have Said Nothing'," in Dene Grigar, Nicholas Schiller, Vanessa Rhodes et al. (eds.), *Rebooting Electronic Literature Volume 1*. Vancouver: Nouspace Publications. https://doi.org/10.7273/NKQK-H488.

(2019) "Curiouser & Curiouser: The Mad House of Kathryn Cramer's *in Small & Large Pieces*," in Dene Grigar, Nicholas Schiller, Vanessa Rhodes et al. (eds.), *Rebooting Electronic Literature Volume 2*. Vancouver: Nouspace Publications. https://scalar.usc.edu/works/rebooting-electronic-literature-volume-2/whoshattered-the-looking-glass-by-astrid-ensslin.

Grigar, Dene and John Barber (2003) "Media Translation Theory and the Online Brautigan Bibliography." *Proceedings from the Digital Arts and Culture 2003*. Ed. Adrian Miles. Melbourne: Royal Melbourne Institute of Technology. CD-ROM Reprinted in *Fineart Forum* 16 (2003).

Grigar, Dene and Stuart Moulthrop (2015) *Pathfinders: Documenting the Experience of Early Digital Literature*. Vancouver: Nouspace Publications. https://doi.org/10.7273/WFoB-TQ14.

Halliday, Michael Alexander Kirkwood and Ruqaiya Hasan (1985) *Language, Context and Text: Aspects of Language in a Social-Semiotic Perspective*. Geelong: Deakin University Press.

Harman, Graham (2005) *Guerrilla Metaphysics: Phenomenology and the Carpentry of Things*. Chicago, IL: Open Court Press.

Harpold, Terry (1998) "Conclusions," in Paula Geyh, Fred G. Leebron, and Andrew Levy (eds.), *Postmodern American Fiction*. New York: W. W. Norton, 637–648.

(2009) *Ex-foliations: Reading Machines and the Upgrade Path*. Minnesota, MN: The University of Minnesota Press.

Hayles, N. Katherine (2000) "Flickering Connectivities in Shelley Jackson's *Patchwork Girl*: The Importance of Media-Specific Analysis," *Postmodern Culture: Journal of Interdisciplinary thought on Contemporary Culture*.

www.pomoculture.org/2013/09/19/flickering-connectivities-in-shelley-jack sonspatchwork-girl-the-importance-of-media-specific-analysis/.

(2002) *Writing Machines*. Cambridge, MA: The MIT Press.

(2003) "Translating Media: Why We Should Rethink Textuality," *The Yale Journal of Criticism* 16(2): 263–290.

(2005) *My Mother Was a Computer: Digital Subjects and Literary Texts*. Chicago, IL: The University of Chicago Press.

(2007) "Electronic Literature: What Is It?" *Electronic Literature Organization*. https://eliterature.org/pad/elp.html.

(2012) *How We Think: Digital Media and Contemporary Technogen*esis. Chicago, IL: The University of Chicago Press.

(2017) *Unthought: The Power of the Cognitive Nonconscious*. Chicago, IL: The University of Chicago Press.

(2022) Interview. *The NEXT*. https://the-next.eliterature.org/works/1983/ 40/0/.

Jobs, Steve (2010) "Thoughts on Flash." https://web.archive.org/web/ 20170615060422/https://www.apple.com/hotnews/thoughtson-flash/.

Johnson, Mark (1987) *The Body in the Mind: The Bodily Basis of Meaning, Imagination, and Reason*. Chicago, IL: The University of Chicago Press.

Jones, Caroline A. (2006) "Introduction," in Carolyn A. Jones (ed.), *Sensorium: Embodied Experience, Technology, and Contemporary Art*. Cambridge, MA: The MIT Press, 5–49.

Joyce, Michael (2016) Email to Dene Grigar. May 31.

(1992) Letter to Sandra Kroups. May 25.

(1995) *Of Two Minds: Hypertext Pedagogy and Poetics*. Ann Arbor, MI: The University of Michigan Press.

(2020a) Email to Dene Grigar. June 4.

(2020b) Email to Dene Grigar. June 5.

(2022c) Email to Dene Grigar. June 18.

Katan, David (2018) "'Translatere' or 'Transcreare': Theory and in Practice, and by Whom?," in Cinzia Spinzi, Alessandra Rizzo, and Marianna Lya Zummo (eds.), *Translation or Transcreation: Discourses, Texts, and Visuals*. Newcastle upon Tyne: Cambridge Scholars Press, 15–38.

Keeley, Edmund (1989) "Collaboration, Revision, and Other Less Forgiveable Sins," in John Biguenet and Rainer Schulte (eds.), *The Craft of Translation*. Chicago, IL: The University of Chicago Press, 54–69.

Kendall, Robert and Jean-Hugues Réty (2005) "Word Circuits Connection Muse User's Guide Version 1.0," www.wordcircuits.com/connect/doc& tools/1-0/manual.htm.

Kirchenbaum, Matthew (2002) "Editing the Interface: Textual Studies and First Generation Electronic Objects," *Text: An Interdisciplinary Annual of Textual Studies* 14: 15–51.

(2008) *Mechanisms: New Media and the Forensic Imagination.* Cambridge, MA: The MIT Press.

(2012) *Mechanisms: New Media and the Forensic Imagination.* Paperback. Cambridge, MA: The MIT Press.

Krause, Rolf D. (2020a) Email to Dene Grigar. June 16.

(2020b) Email to Dene Grigar. June 18.

(2020c) Email to Dene Grigar. June 23.

Laurel, Brenda (1993) *Computers as Theatre.* Reading, MA: Addison-Wesley.

Levy, David M. (2000) "Where's Waldo? Reflections on Copies and Authenticity in a Digital Environment, in Charles T. Cullen, Peter B. Hirtle, David Levy, Clifford A.

Lynch, and Jeff Rothenberg (eds.), *Authenticity in a Digital Environment.* Washington, DC: Council on Library and Information Resources, 24–31.

Lynch, Patrick J. (1994) "Visual Design for the User Interface Part 1: Design Fundamentals," *Journal of Biocommunications* 21(1): 22–30, http://trantor.sheridanc.on.ca/sys32a1/manual/appendix/gui1.html.

Malloy, Judy (2015) "Traversal of *Uncle Roger*," in Dene Grigar and Stuart Moulthrop (eds.), *Pathfinders:Documenting the Experience of Early Digital Literature.* Vancouver: Nouspace Publications. https://scalar.usc.edu/works/pathfinders/malloys-traversal.

(2018) "Traversal of *Its Name Was Penelope*," in Grigar, Schiller et al. (eds.), *Rebooting Electronic Literature Volume 1.* Vancouver: Nouspace Publications. https://scalar.usc.edu/works/rebooting-electronicliterature/traversal-of-judy-malloys-its-name-was-penelope?path=judy-malloys-its-name-waspenelope.

(2020) "Notes on the Creation of *Its Name Was Penelope*," https://people.well.com/user/jmalloy/statement.html.

Manovich, Lev (2001) *The Language of New Media.* Cambridge, MA: The MIT Press.

(2005) "Generation Flash." In Gerhard M. Buurman (ed.) *Total Interaction*, New York: Springer, 66–77.

Marecki, Piotr and Nick Montfort (2017) "Renderings: Translating Literary Works in the Digital Age." *Digital Scholarship in the Humanities* 32. suppl1: i84–i91. https://academic.oup.com/dsh/article-pdf/32/suppl1/i84/17751533/fqx010.pdf.

McCorduck, Patricia (1991) *Whole Earth Review*, No. 70, Spring, 101.

McDaid, John (2015) in Dene Grigar and Stuart Moulthrop (eds.), "John McDaid Interview, Part 2," *Pathfinders: Documenting the Experience of Early Digital Literature*. https://vimeo.com/112474735.

Mencía, María, Søren Pold and Manuel Portela (2018) "Electronic Literature Translation: Translation as Process, Experience and Mediation," *Electronic Book Review*, May 30, https://doi.org/10.7273/wa3v-ab22., www.electronicbookreview.com/thread/electropoetics/translative.

Merleau-Ponty, Maurice (2012) *Phenomenology of Perception*. Trans. Donald A. Landes. New York: Routledge.

Meza, Nohelia (2017) *New Forms of Literariness in Electronic Literature: An Approach to Rhetorical Enunciation and Temporality*. www.tdx.cat/handle/10803/442967.

Montfort, Nick (2018) "Minding the Electronic Literature Translation Gap." *Electronic Book Review*, August 5. https://electronicbookreview.com/essay/minding-the-electronic-literaturetranslation-gap/.

Moulthrop, Stuart (2022) "READ ME (and How)" [An Introduction to the Web ed] in *Victory Garden*, https://victory-garden2022.com/readME.html.

Moulthrop, Stuart and Dene Grigar (2017) *Traversals: The Use of Preservation for Early Electronic Writing*. Cambridge, MA: The MIT Press.

Murray, Janet (1997) *Hamlet on the Holodeck: The Future of Narrative in Cyberspace*. New York: Free Press.

Nelson, Ted (1999) "Xanalogical Structure, Needed Now More Than Ever: Parallel Documents, Deep Links to Content, Deep Versioning, and Deep Re-use," *ACM Computing Surveys* 31(4): 33, https://doi.org/10.1145/345966.346033.

Ong, Walter (1982) *Orality and Literacy: The Technologizing of the Word*. New York: Routledge Press.

Paul, Christiane (2007) "The Myth of Immateriality: Presenting and Preserving New Media," in Oliver Grau (ed.), *MediaArtHistories*, pp. 251–274. Cambridge, MA: The MIT Press.

Pisarski, Mariusz (2012) "From Storyspace to Browsers. Translating *afternoon, a story* into Polish." *Colloques de l'Université Paris8*, https://octaviana.fr/document/COLN11_5#?c=0&m=0&s=0&cv=0.

Regnauld, Arnaud (2014) "Translating '*afternoon, a story*' by Michael Joyce, or How to Inhabit a Spectral Body," *ELO Conference: Chercher le Texte*, Vancouver: Nouspace Publications.

Rembowska-Płuciennik, Magdalena (2012). Poetyka Intersubiektywności: Kognitywistyczna Teoria Narracji a Proza Xx Wieku. Wydawnictwo Naukowe Uniwersytetu Mikołaja Kopernika.

Rettberg, Scott (2019) *Electronic Literature*. Cambridge: Polity Press.

Rosenberg, Jim (1996) "The Structure of Hypertext Activity." *Proceedings of the Seventh ACM Conference on Hypertext*. New York: ACM, 22–30.

Rumsey, Abby Smith (2016) *When We Are No More: How Memory Is Shaping Our Future*. New York: Bloomsbury

Salter, Anastasia and John Murray (2014) *Flash: Building the Interactive Web*. Cambridge, MA: The MIT Press.

Shillingsburg, Peter L. (1991) "Text as Matter, Concept, and Action," *Studies in Bibliography* 44: 31–82.

Skains, Lyle (2022) "(People Who Identify as) Women in ELit: Nevertheless, We Persist." *ELO Conference*.

Spinzi, Cinzia (2021) "The Wheres, Whats, and Whys of Transcreation," in Cinzia Spinzi, Allessandra Rizzo, and Marianna Lya Zummo (eds.), *Translation or Transcreation: Discourses, Texts and Visuals*. Newcastle upon Tyne: Cambridge Scholars Press, 1–14.

Strickland, Stephanie (2019) "Traversal of *True North*," in Dene Grigar, Nicholas Schiller, Vanessa Rhodes et al. (eds.), *Rebooting Electronic Literature Volume 2*. Vancouver: Nouspace Publications https://scalar .usc.edu/works/rebooting-electronicliterature-volume-2/traversal-of-stephanie-stricklands-true-north.

(1997) "Poetry in the Electronic Environment," *Electronic Book Review*, https://electronicbookreview.com/essay/poetry-in-the-electronic-environ ment/.

Tabbi, Joseph (2003) "Stephanie Strickland's *True North*: A Migration between Media," in Jan Van Looy and Jan Baetens (eds.), *Close Reading New Media: Analyzing Electronic Literature*. Leuven, BE: Leuven University Press, 27–38.

Toadvine, Ted (2019) "Maurice Merleau-Ponty," in Edward N. Zalta (ed.), *The Stanford Encyclopedia of Philosophy*, Spring ed. https://plato.stanford .edu/archives/spr2019/entries/merleau-ponty/.

Tosca, Susanna Pajares (1999) "The Lyrical Quality of Links." *Proceedings of the Seventh ACM Conference on Hypertext and Hypermedia*, New York: ACM, 22–30.

Tremblay-Gaudette, Gabriel (2021) "You Can't Go Home Again: Moving Afternoon Forward through Translation, R. Desjardins, Claire Larsonneur, Philippe Lacour (eds.), *When Translation Goes Digital, Palgrave Studies in Translating and Interpreting*, https://doi.org/10.1007/978-3-030-51761-8_4".

Vanderhaeghe, Stéphane (2013) "Translating the Virtual. '*afternoon, a story*' by Michael Joyce," *ELO Conference*. Paris: Chercher le Texte.

Vannini, Walter (2020) Email to Dene Grigar. July 13.

Varela, Francisco J., Evan Thompson, and Eleanor Rosch (1991) *The Embodied Mind: Cognitive Science and Human Expression*. Cambridge, MA: The MIT Press.

Zielinski, Sigfried, Weibel Peter, Daniel Irrgang (eds.) (2016) *Flusseriana. An Intellectual Toolbox*. Berlin: Univocal.

Cambridge Elements ☰

Digital Literary Studies

Katherine Bode
Australian National University
Katherine Bode is Professor of Literary and Textual Studies at the Australian National University. Her research explores the critical potential and limitations of computational approaches to literature, in publications including *A World of Fiction: Digital Collections and the Future of Literary History* (2018), *Advancing Digital Humanities: Research, Methods, Theories* (2014), *Reading by Numbers: Recalibrating the Literary Field* (2012), and *Resourceful Reading: The New Empiricism, eResearch and Australian Literary Culture* (2009).

Adam Hammond
University of Toronto
Adam Hammond is Assistant Professor of English at the University of Toronto. He is author of *Literature in the Digital Age* (Cambridge 2016) and co-author of *Modernism: Keywords* (2014). He works on modernism, digital narrative, and computational approaches to literary style. He is editor of the forthcoming *Cambridge Companion to Literature in the Digital Age* and *Cambridge Critical Concepts: Literature and Technology*.

Gabriel Hankins
Clemson University
Gabriel Hankins is Associate Professor of English at Clemson University. His first book is *Interwar Modernism and the Liberal World Order* (Cambridge 2019). He writes on modernism, digital humanities, and color. He is technical manager for the *Twentieth Century Literary Letters Project* and co-editor of *The Digital Futures of Graduate Study in the Humanities* (in progress).

Advisory Board

David Bammen, *University of California, Berkeley*
Amy Earhardt, *Texas A&M University*
Dirk Van Hulle, *University of Oxford*
Fotis Jannidis, *Julius-Maximilians-Universität*
Matthew Kirschenbaum, *University of Maryland*
Laura Mandell, *Texas A&M University*
Élika Ortega-Guzman, *University of Colorado, Boulder*
Marisa Parham, *Amherst College*
Rita Raley, *University of California, Santa Barbara*
Scott Rettberg, *University of Bergen*
Roopika Risam, *Salem State University*
Glenn Roe, *Sorbonne University*
Whitney Trettien, *University of Pennsylvania*
Ted Underwood, *University of Illinois*

About the Series
Our series provides short exemplary texts that address a pressing research question of clear scholarly interest within a defined area of literary studies, clearly articulate the method used to address the question, and demonstrate the literary insights achieved.

Cambridge Elements $^{\equiv}$

Digital Literary Studies

Printed in the United States
by Baker & Taylor Publisher Services